Sunshine and Ice

Volume 9

DIAMONDS AND GOLD

MARTIN MONEY

All paper used in the printing of this book has been made from wood
grown in managed, sustainable forests.

ISBN 978-1-78003-840-7

Printed and published in the UK

Author Essentials Ltd
4 The Courtyard
South Street
Falmer
East Sussex
BN1 9PQ

A catalogue record of this book is available from
the British Library

Cover design by Jacqueline Abromeit

DIAMONDS AND GOLD

Part One

August and September 2014

INTRODUCTION – THE BLAME GAME

Seems to me we're living in a society where people are guilty until proven innocent. This represents a sick and twisted version of reality and a total reversal of the golden rule I was brought up with and which is still written into the laws of our fair land.

The rise in social networking sites has meant we've gone way beyond trial by TV. It's now a case of pillory anyone you don't like on the internet and destroy their good name without a shred of hard evidence. That's sinister and dangerous in my view.

Harsh comments, cruel jokes and cavalier character assassinations are rife. And those recklessly poisoning communication channels with nasty jibes and spite-fuelled rants are clearly blissfully unaware that they're committing the serious crime of libel that can carry a jail sentence.

The only real defence against a libel action is to prove that what you've claimed is true. Speculation and suspicion don't cut it in court. But most people don't realise this – and newspaper editors with clever and callous lawyers simply don't care.

Cynical Fleet Street hacks are the masters of strong suggestion and clever phrasing that deviously and deliberately misleads readers, enticing them to draw certain conclusions and believe them implicitly in the total absence of hard facts.

These readers, nowhere near as skilled in word manipulation, then repeat the unproven allegations on Facebook or Twitter in a far cruder form without the subtle nuances that keep editors out of prison.

And all this is going on while calls intensify to bring back hanging and other barbaric punishments. Some folk demand extreme treatment of perceived offenders even when there's simply a claim of serious wrongdoing totally untested in a law court.

Innocent people fear violent retribution. I thought we were supposed to be more enlightened, compassionate, civilised and tolerant these days – apparently not.

Sure, wrongdoers need to be stopped. Those inflicting harm on others should be punished in accordance with the severity of their crimes. Their reasons for erring have to be addressed. We all need protection – children, adults and yes, animals too.

I'm well aware that our legal system isn't perfect. And I know it can be exploited by the shrewd and unscrupulous to frame and lock up the innocent while the guilty walk free. But on the whole I firmly support it, and especially the major tenet that someone's deemed to be innocent until proven otherwise in court.

I've had my own deeply personal reasons to be cynical. At one time I was furious at the way I was treated by that very legal system. But I've since come to regain my trust in a setup that generally upholds my ingrained instincts for fairness and justice.

Hypocrisy is rampant as we eagerly slate others, ignoring our own flaws, failings and foul-ups. We've all done wrong in various degrees and no-one is perfect. We'd do well to remember that…

CHAPTER ONE – HELLO OLD FRIEND

August 10, 2014 – Well, the Bell re-launch day was a resounding success. I went along for the lunchtime opening ceremony and then stayed on for a few pints, leaving mid-afternoon.

By then it was starting to get busy and I hear that during the evening it became quite crowded as a party atmosphere prevailed – probably a bit too hectic for my liking.

Bournemouth Mayor Councillor Chris Mayne unveiled the Bell sign to start a fun-packed all day event.

A bouncy castle, mechanical rodeo bull, mini steam trains, life-sized dalek, blow-up "gladiators" arena, fancy dress costumes, barbeque, live music and a deejay were among the attractions.

Children and dogs were much in evidence during the family-orientated daytime session before the booze and dance crowd took over for the evening hours. By all accounts, it was a total triumph.

New couple in charge Mark Evans and Laura Williams have done a grand job turning the pub back into a proper "local" after five years of it being just a building where people drank.

I wish them all the success in the world. It was great seeing the new landlord and landlady joining their staff in trying out the fun activities, all really getting into the celebratory spirit.

It's nice to see people enjoying themselves at work while still doing their jobs with care, good humour and efficiency.

And for me, it was like welcoming back a dear old friend following a forced absence. After all, it's been my pub for the past 20 years even though it's not felt much like it of late – until now.

Thanks to Laura and Mark, all that's changing again, or rather, getting back to the way it should be. Sweet!

August 11 – It's Laura's 21st birthday today. Here's hoping she has a great one!

On the news, fighting continues in the Ukraine, Iraq and Syria but a fragile ceasefire's being observed in the Gaza strip. And MPs here are calling for health warnings to be put on bottles and cans of alcoholic drink. Not a bad idea in my view.

I take the same attitude to this as labelling food, tobacco and other products. If people are told what's in them, the possible health risks and the processes by which they've been brought from natural state to shop shelf, they then have all the relevant data enabling them to make an informed choice as to whether to buy and consume or not.

Having said that, when warning of potential health hazards we shouldn't be too alarmist. Just state the facts calmly, clearly and concisely and leave folk to make up their own minds. Being too graphic and gruesome just disgusts and repels people without necessarily persuading them to use caution or moderation. Maybe the reverse.

Like I've said before, I detest those ridiculously over-the-top, in your face TV adverts using shock tactics that make people cringe and laugh nervously while totally failing to get important and potentially life-saving points across.

Especially when so much hard cash flowing into government coffers is at stake.

I do think it's two-faced and more than a bit rich for MPs to issue such health warnings while apparently being quite happy to relieve individuals of their money in the form of taxes on booze and cigarettes.

Let's face it – the government would lose millions in revenue overnight and wouldn't be too pleased if everyone actually took such advice seriously and gave up drinking and smoking tomorrow. Such bold hypocrisy really sticks in my craw.

And there's no guarantee consumers would take any notice of health risk data anyway. But at least they couldn't then complain they weren't warned if they did subsequently fall ill. So I still think the idea's worth pursuing.

August 12 – Oscar-winning American actor and comedian Robin Williams has died aged 63. It is thought he might have taken his own life after a bout of depression.

He shot to fame in the late 1970s and early 1980s playing a zany and amiable alien in the smash hit US television sitcom *Mork and Mindy*. He then went on to star in many massively-successful films.

He won his Academy award for *Good Will Hunting* and was one of those skilled guys who could mix comedy and pathos in equal measure, making us laugh and cry all at the same time.

My own personal favourites were *Dead Poets' Society*, *Patch Adams*, *Good Morning Vietnam* and *Hook*, where he played a grown-up Peter Pan opposite Dustin Hoffman's Captain Hook.

I had that film on video and watched it numerous times with my son Phil – then still just a boy. We both loved it.

Others will list *Jumanji*, *Popeye*, *Flubber*, *Mrs Doubtfire*, *What Dreams May Come*, *Toys* or *Night at the Museum* among their top movies. He was universally loved as a very funny and entertaining man both on and off screen. He was brilliant at stand-up.

Tributes have poured in for this immensely talented and versatile guy who was apparently a lovely bloke as well.

US President Barack Obama said: "Williams arrived in our lives as an alien – but he ended up touching every element of the human spirit.

"He made us laugh. He made us cry. He gave his immeasurable talent freely and generously to those who needed it most – from our troops stationed abroad to the marginalised on our own streets."

That's quite an accolade which will be warmly supported the world over. Williams was an icon, a legend, and will be sorely missed.

It's turning into a pretty sad, bad summer for prematurely losing superbly talented funny men, what with Rik Mayall's shock demise at only 56 in June.

How we desperately need such stars to brighten our lives, making us smile and think.

August 13 – And another one bites the dust! Williams' fellow movie legend Lauren Bacall has also passed on – in her case, at her New York home after apparently suffering a stroke. She was 89.

Bacall is probably best known for her screen partnership with husband Humphrey Bogart in such film classics as *Key Largo*, *Dark Passage* and *The Big Sleep*.

Her Hollywood career spanned seven decades, with a memorable debut in 1944 aged just 19 opposite Bogart in *To Have and Have Not*. Her outstanding performance, husky voice and smouldering looks made her an instant star.

They married the following year and had two children together. Bogart died in 1957. She had another child with her second husband, actor Jason Robards, and also had a brief romance with Frank Sinatra.

Five decades into her career, she picked up a Golden Globe award and was nominated for an Oscar in 1996 after appearing in *The Mirror Has Two Faces* with Barbra Streisand and Jeff Bridges.

Bacall collected an honorary Academy award in 2009 in recognition of "her central place in the golden age of motion pictures".

On the home front, monthly figures put out by the government show a fall in unemployment and a steadily improving economy. Well there's a surprise!

Politicians and number crunchers continue to inhabit their dream world of deliberately distorted data, talking blithely of progress while millions suffer in a different reality, trying to pick up the pieces of the devastation they've caused.

You know, the reality of closed firms, a scandalous scarcity of genuine, lasting paid work opportunities, of rising prices and cutbacks in essential services and welfare payments. Of homelessness, runaway debts, forced labour with no wages, food banks, hardship, poverty and misery.

Many people round these parts would love to swap places – lifestyle-wise – with the arrogant, uncaring Dave, George and Nick. How about it, boys? – thought not!

August 18 – Happy anniversary to my sister Carol and hubby David, who married 41 years ago today. Also to my good friends Jeff and Tina McNally, who tied the knot exactly 13 years ago.

It's always nice to see couples staying together for years, whether married or not. I feel that such stability is good for society as a whole – especially when children are involved.

And I say that as someone whose own marriage lasted just seven years, and whose son was three when it ended.

Of course, any couple needs to be relatively happy – not bound by the old convention that miserable people should stay together "for the kids' sake", a mad idea which actually did the youngsters a lot more harm than good by forcing them to grow up in homes full of friction, coldness and resentment.

Many people choose not to commit to long-term relationships. Others seem to drift from one partner to another without settling down with anyone. Fine, so long as everyone involved understands the situation and such scenarios are played out with the minimum of hurt and suffering.

I just think it's better for our communities when citizens are settled and reasonably content with their home arrangements and children grow up in supportive environments full of love and calm.

And I make no distinction here between same sex and heterosexual relationships.

But getting back to Jeff McNally, I actually saw him face to face last night for the first time in a while. He popped in to the Bell and it was good to have a catch-up.

John Gaynor, John Palmer, Lee Robertson, Bev Jones, Tim Robbins, Vicky Brown and her feller Mark were also there, my friend Sam Rose Lowney was behind the bar and her husband Dave turned up later. New managers Laura and Mark flitted about, mingling with punters.

It was another highly satisfactory karaoke evening in my local pub, finishing off a good weekend of booze, friendship and silliness.

Saturday I was invited to my good mates Sam and Carl's place for a few pleasant hours with them, their sons Rudy and Bailey, Sam's daughter Becca, her dad and Sam's ex-partner Russell, Jem Hannen, Tina Mcauley and Jimmy.

Family dogs Albert, a terrier, and Blaze, a lovely sweet-natured Staffie, were also there, along with Blaze's pups, off to their new homes soon.

August 20 – Have dreams by all means, son, but always make sure you've got a bread and butter job to pay the bills. This sterling piece of advice was given to the teenage me by my wise father.

But the emphasis was very much on the second part of the sentence. These were the days when so-called ordinary people were positively discouraged from taking gambles in search of happiness.

Dad came from a generation that had known world war, grim lifestyles, hard attitudes and limited choices. He left school at 14 with no paper qualifications, desperate to earn a wage to help support his struggling family.

He ended up doing a variety of jobs – including door-to-door insurance salesman, welder and caretaker – to earn much-needed cash. If he started off with dreams and ambitions, stark reality would have forced him to ditch them pretty damned quickly.

Millions of working class people like Dad simply didn't have that luxury of choice. It was financial sink or swim with no welfare state safety nets.

So I don't blame him for phrasing his advice as he did – playing down the dream bit and stressing the need to feed, house and clothe myself.

And it was my fault, not his, that I timidly toed the line, lacking both courage and a clarity of purpose. I should have been more assertive, with a far sharper vision of where I wanted to go and a practical plan of how to get there.

Instead, I spent most of my time harbouring vague ideals while floundering about with little or no sense of purpose, reacting to events and developments rather than instigating them, screwing up and getting disillusioned.

Eventually, quite recently, I at last found my station. I got here in the end after decades of hassle, uncertainty, frustration and disappointment. But that was thanks to my dear departed sister Jan, not any determined or well-defined efforts on my part.

It's pathetic really – and ironic, considering the opportunities I had that my Dad didn't and the faith my immediate family placed in me that, as the youngest in changing times with new horizons opening up, I'd be the one to break the mould and climb further out of the hard-edged rut we all lived in.

(My parents were overjoyed that I was the first of their children to get A-levels, while my cousin Colin became the real Money family high-flyer by getting a degree.)

But then, that faith was very much tempered by a stubbornly persistent old school paradigm that warned against being too reckless and adventurous in risking all for the sake of probably unachievable goals.

Modes of thinking have changed over the years and modern youth is encouraged to chase dreams while being presented with a much wider range of choices and opportunities. Or at least, it has been.

Now, with education standards falling again, a marked scarcity of proper career opportunities and little job security any longer, I fear we're steadily returning to the bad old days. And I find that highly undesirable and pretty damned alarming.

August 21 – Happy first birthday Roxanna, daughter of Phil's step-sister Alison and her feller Terry. And a happy 50th to my mate Andy Frend.

On a sadder note, it's eight years ago today that Sam's dad Jim Excell passed on. I'm going round her place later to raise a glass – well, can of lager – in his memory.

August 24, 6pm – Earlier today I had a fab few hours with the family. Phil and Emily brought my grandkids Chloe (15 months) and Lucas, three, over to see me and we all went through wooded Fisherman's Walk to a children's play park on Southbourne cliff top.

It was great fun and Chloe and Lucas thoroughly enjoyed it (Harvey was with Em's parents). Chloe, who's walking now, beamed at me continuously and Lucas asked me to push him on a swing and share a seesaw, which was really cool. What treasured memories in the making!

Changing the subject completely, I've just heard some unsettling news on the football front. Manchester United's second game of their Premier League campaign finished minutes ago with them drawing 1-1 with Sunderland.

They lost their first match last weekend against Swansea, so have picked up only one point from a possible six – not a very impressive start for new manager Louis van Gaal.

Hopes were high after he led the Dutch national team to finish third in this summer's World Cup tournament in Brazil. He has won trophies with teams in three different countries. Let's hope he can turn it around pretty damned quick at Old Trafford!

My home team Bournemouth, by contrast, have had an encouraging start to their new season. They won their first two league games and briefly sat proudly atop the Championship table. Okay, they lost their next two and have slipped to 11th, but there's still only four points between them and current leaders Nottingham Forest.

Meanwhile, flesh-biting footballer Luis Suárez has left Liverpool for Barcelona. But the Uruguayan won't be playing for a while as he's currently serving a four-month ban from all soccer-related activities after sinking his teeth into an Italian defender's shoulder during a World Cup game.

August 25 – Blimey! Famous people are dropping like flies at the moment. The latest to pass on is legendary film-maker Richard Attenborough, aged 90.

Lord Attenborough was one of Britain's leading character actors during the middle of last century before becoming a highly successful director.

His first film role was playing a cowardly sailor in the much-acclaimed 1942 war movie *In Which We Serve*, starring Noel Coward and John Mills.

Versatile Attenborough could play parts from serial killer John Christie in *10 Rillington Place* to an avuncular guy who thinks he's Santa Claus in *Miracle on 34th Street*.

Other acting successes came in such classic films as *Brighton Rock*, *The Great Escape* and *Jurassic Park*. Directorial credits included *Gandhi*, which earned him two Oscars, *A Bridge Too Far* and *Cry Freedom*, about the death of South African anti-apartheid campaigner Steven Biko.

He's credited with almost single-handedly rescuing the British film industry when it faced eclipse by America. An avid Labour Party man, he passionately championed social justice and headed campaigns helping muscular dystrophy sufferers.

He was said to be a very kind man and tributes have poured in. Surviving younger brother David, 88, is equally revered globally as a naturalist and wildlife film maker.

August 26 – Wishing a very happy birthday to my mate Claire Kimber. I sent her a text earlier today (she's not on Facebook).

Readers of my previous books will know that Claire worked behind the bar at the Bell for several years and was the first new friend I made when I started going there in a bid to rebuild my social life after my marriage broke up in the early 1990s.

She used to drive me and other mates to the Bournemouth night spots like Poets' Corner, Park Lane and the Exchange. She also drove on various excursions arranged among pub regulars. Lots of sweet memories!

Speaking of mates, I've recently been remembering some of the fine times I had with my best pal growing up, Steve Mitchell. No idea why, but that's recollections for you – they pop into your head for no apparent reason at random times as you go about your day.

He lived just round the corner to my home in Slough. We met at infants' school and then went to juniors' together. But on both passing our 11-plus exams, we were gutted to be forced apart because our parents had chosen different high schools for us. But we still saw each other at weekends.

On one classic occasion, we got on our bikes one Saturday morning in September to ride to the local outdoor swimming pool about three miles away. It was just a couple of weeks before it closed for the winter.

We endured rain, thunder and lightning but were determined to go through with it. On arriving at the lido, we discovered we were the only two people there. As we paid our entrance fee and walked to the changing rooms, we heard a bored lifeguard say to the ticket office guy: "Crazy kids!"

Once in the water, it was great fun and not too cold so we had a brilliant time with the pool to ourselves. But on getting out and changing to leave, we felt decidedly chilly and needed cups of Bovril to warm us up. Crazy kids indeed!

Steve was a very good guitarist and encouraged me to try my hand. Trouble was, I lacked the persistence to practise for hours like he did and I gave up pretty fast.

He started aged nine with an acoustic guitar his parents bought. Developing his skills, he got better ones, quickly switching to electric and ending up the proud owner of a beautiful Gibson Les Paul that was a joy to handle. The craftsmanship was superb.

I did eventually learn the basics of simple guitar chords on joining amateur gospel/pop group the Dominoes (see my earlier books).

But by starting early and persevering, Steve had got so good by young adulthood he could well have gone professional and in fact was briefly in a rock group called Liar, formed in Maidenhead in 1975 by Dave Taylor.

Bassist Taylor was previously with pop group Edison Lighthouse, who had hit number one in the UK singles charts in 1970 with a song called Love Grows Where My Rosemary Grows.

I went to see Steve with Liar once at a pub in Maidenhead called the Bell – yes I know, strange coincidence innit?

The band went off to America to try and make it but Steve chose to quit so he could pursue a career as a wine-taster – well-paid regular work far less reliant on notoriously fickle fortune.

I lost contact with him when he went abroad – Spain I think – and I moved from Slough to Dorset.

Meanwhile, Liar did indeed make it as a rock band, touring internationally and supporting top-rated acts like Slade and UFO.

As a journalist I got hold of a vinyl copy of Liar's second album Set the World on Fire (1978) and reviewed it for the *Poole Herald* just after moving from Slough.

It was a good record containing a track called Five Knuckle Shuffle, co-written by Steve and Dave Taylor.

The album was well received in the US, sold steadily and reached third place in the Billboard airplay charts behind Bob Dylan's Street Legal and Who Are You by the Who. Cool! – and a nice royalty cheque for my mate, no doubt.

I often wonder where Steve is now and what he's up to. He certainly could have been a successful rock musician had he stayed with Liar.

The above brief trip down memory lane takes us up to 1978 when I moved down to Dorset. Shortly after relocating, I met Sharon – Shaz, my "faith healer" – a really close mate and one of the few people I befriended in Bournemouth who met and would remember my parents and our old home in New Park Road, Southbourne.

Dad adored this attractive, bubbly, flirty Barnsley lass. He was particularly amused by her audacity. She would turn up at our door saying things like "you got that kettle on? I'm parched" or "what's in the fridge? I'm starving."

That was Shaz, cheeky, friendly and funny – a diamond person and cherished pal who helped me sort my head out many times using her remarkable perception and wisdom. Bless her! I similarly often wonder what became of her since she returned home to Yorkshire a few years back.

Over the decades I've accumulated many other fond memories of treasured times with good friends. I still am of course. But Steve and Shaz are two I've been thinking about lately after losing touch with them years ago.

August 26, evening – I've just seen an item on the TV news about Kate Bush returning to the stage later tonight after a 35-year break.

14

She hasn't played live since her first and only tour ended at London's Hammersmith Apollo in 1979.

Awarded a CBE for her services to music, she's returning to the same venue for 22 dates – all sold out within minutes of tickets being made available in March.

Now 56, the doctor's daughter from Kent started writing songs when she was only 11 and had already written over 100 when she came to the notice of Pink Floyd's Dave Gilmour when she was 16. A recording contract quickly followed.

One of Britain's most influential and enigmatic artists, she shot to fame when her song Wuthering Heights hit the UK singles top spot in 1978.

At 19, she was the first solo female to have a UK number one with a self-penned song and the record also topped the charts in Ireland and Italy and became a big hit in several other European countries.

Like many, I remember being blown away on first seeing her, performing Wuthering Heights on Top of the Pops. She was electrifying, brilliant, totally original and like a breath of fresh air – clearly a major new talent.

Our Kate did just one tour before quitting live performances but continued to make outstanding and groundbreaking hit albums and had several other successful singles over the years. She remained adventurous and thought-provoking throughout.

She's well respected in the music business by everyone from Elton John to John Lydon. She's influenced many artists who sing her praises.

I love her and think she's a genius – the whole package. An attractive, charismatic, mysterious and mesmerising woman who's a superb songwriter, singer, dancer, producer and multi-instrumentalist.

In short, she's my favourite female music star of all time. Welcome back Kate, good luck for your live shows girl.

August 27 – Well done AFC Bournemouth, who last night beat Northampton 3-0 in the second round of the League Cup. But oh dear Manchester United – thrashed 4-0 by League One side MK Dons in the same competition.

After learning of this new instalment of van Gaal's nightmare, I cheered myself up by tuning in to watch two back-to-back episodes of the excellent TV sitcom Two Pints of Lager and a Packet of Crisps, being shown on the Viva Channel.

I'm a keen fan of this sharp, witty, funny and occasionally quite surreal TV show. I particularly love the first musical episode When Janet met Jonny, a between-series special sadly not shown on telly.

It's wonderful from start to finish with terrific Mickey-takes of hit pop songs. All the cast excel and it's obvious they're having great fun.

Then it was over to BBC Three for the animated comedy shows Family Guy and American Dad, two of the best programmes to come out of America in recent years,

They're also very clever, witty and funny with hilariously random moments.

Yes, I'm a telly addict – and I don't apologize for that. It gives me a lot of enjoyment.

But now I feel it's time to turn from entertainment to politics – yes, again! But only briefly.

I've already said that although I detest the cold, harsh form of capitalism by which our country's run, I do believe there is a far more compassionate version I for one would be a lot happier with.

And recently I've been looking again at the idea of co-operatives – organisations that give power to the people. Workers have a say in running co-operative businesses and banks, consumers have a vote where retail outlets are involved, farmers where food groups are concerned.

Of course, the Co-op dairy group, supermarket chain, banking business and funeral parlour network are four of the most famous examples. The John Lewis Partnership and its subsidiary Waitrose are others.

This, I feel, is an excellent idea which ties in nicely with my vision of a more caring type of capitalism tempered with strong aspects of democratic liberal, socialist and above all green sensibilities.

August 28 – Happy birthday to my mate Simon "Squeak" Turnbull, who recently got married.

Yesterday I spent a few hours round Sam and Carl's with them, Rudy, Bailey, Sam's cousin Diane –who I remember from the old Home Guard Social Club days – Jem Hannen, Sharon Pendleton and the family dogs Albert and Blaze.

Blaze is off to live with Sam's ex-partner Russell in a few days' time. We'll all miss her terribly as she's a lovely, placid-natured Staffie, but it's better for her to go to Russ, who's in a position to devote more time and attention to her.

Homes have been found for all Blaze's puppies now including a female, Milly, who's going to Russell's with her mum.

August 30 – Watched some old episodes of another telly classic last night – Father Ted on the More 4 Channel. It's wonderful – superbly written and acted, very funny with that touch of surreal weirdness I love in a comedy show.

The highly original sitcom, relating the hilarious capers of three Irish priests, their equally oddball colleagues and their overzealous housekeeper, has quite rightly won awards and become the stuff of legend.

Former teacher Dermot Morgan (Father Ted) was a mighty fine comic talent and it's a great shame he died of a heart attack so young – 45. It makes us wonder what else he might have achieved had he lived longer.

Frank Kelly (Father Jack) was already established and Ardal O-Hanlon (Father Dougal), Pauline McLynn (Mrs Doyle) and Graham Norton (Father Furlong) all went on to enjoy highly successful careers.

The three series of Father Ted were comedy gold.

And speaking of gold, it's my great mate Jem Hannen's 50th birthday today. Greetings and salutations buddy – have a fab one!

As I've already said, it's quite a year for landmark birthdays – Jem, Carl, Andy and Russell have all recently had their fiftieths. Joe and Cheryl mark theirs in October.

So I guess they're all about to live through their golden years.

Back in February, I joined the ranks of the diamond days fraternity by reaching my sixtieth.

Diamond days and golden years. Yeah, I like that – diamonds and gold.

Turning briefly to more serious matters, the UK has apparently been put on high alert for terrorist attack in light of the worsening situations in the Middle East and Ukraine and a perceived threat of violent Islamic militancy going global and reaching us here.

Well, that's what happens I guess when our political leaders slate foreigners, demonize ethnic groups and meddle in blood-drenched conflicts abroad. They make us a target, just as I've warned. Thanks for nothing fellers!

September 1 – Happy birthday "Danger Mouse" – my mate Paul Dangerfield. We used to drink in the Bell together but now he lives in Wexford, Ireland, with his lady Sarah Basham. They're Facebook friends of mine and we stay in regular contact.

Paul isn't quite entering his golden years – he's 48 today. Neither is another pal Rodney Marlow, who's 49 tomorrow. But my former work colleague and drinking buddy Lorna Lane is 40 at the end of this month, so will be celebrating her ruby birthday.

Other friends have already passed their ruby, gold and diamond milestones. I've always said my mates are treasures!

September 3 – Yesterday was a good 'un. Went to Days Chinese/English restaurant in Bournemouth for a meal with Sam, Carl, the boys, Bec and Tina.

Bec, 18, only just back from her first holiday abroad, then went home to recoup, but the rest of us progressed to the town's shops including HMV.

While there, I picked up CDs by Iggy Azalea, Clean Bandit, Kate Bush, the Arctic Monkeys, Passenger and Peter Tosh. Surweet!

I'm playing Iggy Azalea's album The New Classic as I type this. This 24-year-old Australian lass is one of the new stars of the rap/hip hop genre.

She's a bit like a female Eminem but has been accused of being a racist after apparently making ill-informed comments about Aboriginals.

This may or may not be true, but such allegations aside, she is a bright new talent and I like her music.

The real bargain in my little assortment of new CDs was five albums by reggae star and former Wailer Peter Tosh, all packaged together for £10. Now I need to get some Aswad and Steel Pulse to further boost my humble reggae collection.

Happy birthday Bev Jones, a good female mate of mine for many years. We used to visit each other and whoever was hosting would sort out a meal. Pudding was always jam roly poly, which we both love.

Bev also held weekly wine, chat and laughter evenings for a group of us at her old flat in Boscombe. Occasionally we'd touch on a serious topic, but mainly it was yakking about nonsense.

This was the original Tuesday night club, before my great buddy Steve Yarwood and I used the same title for our weekly booze and silliness sessions a little later.

September 4 – I'm listening to my new Passenger CD, Whispers, as I write this. Earlier today, I played the Arctic Monkeys' album AM, bought at the same time two days ago. Both are excellent.

Mike Rosenberg, aka Passenger, is one heck of a good song writer. His music's good, but I especially like his lyrics – perceptive and poetic with a fresh new twist. And his delivery is superb. The same applies to Alex Turner of the Arctic Monkeys.

These guys are among the cream of the current crop of mighty fine lyricists of both sexes making hit singles and albums. Ed Sheeran, Rita Ora, Ellie Goulding and Jake Bugg are others. Their words and phrasing are imaginative and highly original.

I like good music, but I love great lyrics. Sadly, there are still far too many records in the charts with okay or even terrific music but disappointingly ordinary or even rubbish words. I feel there's been no excuse for this since the trailblazing 1960s.

September 5 – American comedy legend and chat show host Joan Rivers has died aged 81 a week after suffering a heart attack during a routine procedure at a clinic.

A pioneer of late-night TV, she courted both celebrity and controversy with her caustic wit flying in the face of political correctness.

So yet another icon has passed on to the next level. In this respect, it's been a pretty sad few months. It brings home the realization that we all have to go some time, and makes us wonder how long any of us have left.

****

CHAPTER TWO – CONTROL FREAKS

September 6 – Conspiracy theorists will tell you there's an evil organisation hell-bent on running everything and establishing a new world order of brutal fascism in which the rest of us are just slaves.

These despicable control freaks are driven by greed and selfishness – ruthless in their crazed quest to have all the power and wealth.

Bankers, royal families, politicians, establishment big shots and celebrities are among those involved and the agenda is pushed forward using unelected committees and secretive societies such as the Freemasons, claim the theorists.

Readers of my books will know that I think there's a lot of mileage in this idea. It accords with my own view that such as group has been in charge for millennia.

It also explains a lot of mystifying inconsistencies in what we're told and how things are done and have been through history.

Some call this sinister organisation the Illuminati. But I found an internet website yesterday carrying a strong denial of that allegation.

It centred on a fascinating interview with a guy claiming to be part of the Illuminati's ruling council – breaking its strict code of silence to put the record straight, he said.

This feller, whose identity was concealed, told his questioner that the council has 12 members – five Americans, five Western Europeans, a Russian and an Indian.

It was indeed a secretive conspiratorial organisation intent on ushering in a new world order, but its motives were benevolent and it was acting in the interests of mankind.

It numbered fewer than 6,000. And these people didn't worship Mammon, as alleged.

The conspiracy theorists were right in a lot of what they said, but they'd wrongly identified the Illuminati as their enemy.

In fact, the real foe was the old world order – the cash-obsessed establishment – that he and like-minded folk wanted to overthrow thus liberating us all, he asserted.

Religions based on faith that demanded subservience to a deity were a crucial part of that evil and corrupt set-up. The Illuminati held that enlightened knowledge was the key to releasing the divinity lying within each one of us.

In effect, he was saying that he and his peers were the good guys fighting for a better future for all – a future in which humanity evolved to a more divine level, and justice, fairness and equality prevailed: the New World Order.

But to achieve that the current system had to be dismantled. It was run by a merciless network of psychopaths savagely exploiting other people in their self-centred quest for money and power.

You're probably thinking well, he would say that, wouldn't he? And part of me does too. But what he claims is intriguing.

I don't know one way or the other. But I am certain we're all prey to a sinister group running the show from the shadows and manipulating people and events for its own self-obsessed purposes – no matter what it chooses to call itself.

As for the Illuminati, it's no fantastical invention of crackpot theorists but a proven historical fact. An Enlightenment-era secret society bearing that name was founded on May 1, 1776 in Bavaria.

Led by Adam Weishaupt, its stated aims were apparently to oppose superstition, prejudice, religious influence over public life and abuses of state power, and to support women's education and gender equality.

But the group, along with other secret societies, was outlawed after pressure from the Roman Catholic Church. Wikipedia tells us it was permanently disbanded in 1785.

Not so, says the anonymous man claiming to be one of its modern-day leaders. He insists that it carried on and thrived, spreading its message while pursuing its mission in secret so as to avoid the violent wrath of its enemies.

His words are quite convincing and his views on politics and religion accord with mine in many respects – assuming he's being truthful, of course.

September 8 – We're just 10 days away from an historic vote that could split the United Kingdom. Yes, Scotland's about to decide whether to leave the Union or stay.

The knock-on effects of a vote for independence could be numerous and far-reaching for people both sides of the border. The real question is whether this would be a good or bad thing.

Informal polls indicate it's going to be a close result with many voters still undecided.

I saw a live TV debate the other day during which citizens showed great frustration that the politicians seemed more interested in arguing with their opponents than actually giving them vital information enabling them to make an informed choice.

Cameron and his cronies continue using scare tactics, warning of dire consequences for the Scots if they vote to go it alone. Meanwhile, Ed Miliband's feeble contribution has been as effective as an ashtray on a motorbike.

Politicians, eh?

I just hope that, whatever happens our two nations remain firm friends linked by blood, trade and shared values and interests.

If its difficult finding the truth amid all the smoke and mirrors of the Scotland issue, then it's nigh on impossible to sort fact from fiction when trying to ascertain who's actually for us and who's our enemy in the hotly-contested Illuminati debate.

I've been looking at various websites over the past couple of days in a bid to ascertain where I stand. I remain dazed and confused.

Up to now, I've tended to accept the arguments of the anti-Illuminati crowd alleging that this shadowy secretive group is the evil force governing our world and reality as we know it, grabbing all the power and cash while ruthlessly exploiting the rest of us.

But then I came across the article containing the interview with the geezer claiming to be a member of its 12-man ruling council, insisting they were the good guys – the enlightened ones fighting the forces of darkness.

This made me wonder, so I've continued my computer-based investigations.

Most of the sites mentioning the Illuminati are very anti, with wild assertions about cold-blooded shape-shifting reptile rulers, devil-worshippers and generally nasty individuals controlling our world for their own twisted ends.

One of the internet pages listed alleged celebrity Illuminati members past and present including Bob Marley, Jimi Hendrix, Paul McCartney, Bob Dylan, Bono and David Bowie.

Well, I thought, if these guys are or have been involved, count me in!

But seriously though, this gave me real food for thought. If people like them have become members, maybe the feller saying it was a force for good was right after all.

One website asserted that the Beatles were either in the ranks or controlled by others who were. They often used alleged Illuminati symbolism including hand signals such as the "devil horns" beloved of heavy metal fans, the thumbs-up and the okay sign.

The same site repeated the hoary old chestnut about secret messages, some of them satanic, in Beatle songs – especially when played backwards.

Of course, the group themselves loved running tapes of their music and words in reverse, recording them for singles and album tracks. They had great fun doing it.

And they did it even more just to tease people when they realized some folk were finding all sorts of apparently unintended hidden messages in their work.

Certainly, their comments and actions frequently seemed to echo stated Illuminati opinions and policies as outlined by the so-called leader on his web page.

But one incredible and deeply insulting statement on a "Beatles Illuminati" site alleged that they were merely puppets, part of a huge mind control experiment, and someone else wrote their songs for them because there was no way a bunch of young working class lads could have written such profound stuff.

Apart from being ignorant and spiteful, this is factually incorrect. Paul and John were actually middle class and all four were sharp as razors. Lennon's song Working Class Hero was deliberately ironic – although sometimes he played up to that false image.

My great admiration for this rock band is well documented. Were they Illuminati? – It's debatable. But to suggest they were anyone's stooges is quite ludicrous.

I've always loved their terrific music, their quick wit and warm humour, their beliefs and attitudes and their wonderful slant on reality.

These regularly tie in with my own views and stances – and they seem to also overlap with a lot of what the supposed Illuminati leader says on his website.

If I'm re-thinking my own position, it's about the possible nature of the secret society, not the rock group.

But I remain baffled and undecided, keeping my mind open to all possibilities.

It's a constant struggle to find the truth in this world of deliberately-distorted reality. That's why so many people don't bother trying. It's also why I'm a great advocate of heeding intuition and gut instinct.

If something feels right and has the ring of authenticity, use it as your viewpoint until another revelation challenges or demolishes it.

Wisdom and enlightenment come as new information reaches us. Only a fool stays rigidly and permanently fixed to an old paradigm in defiance of evolving truth.

David Icke is one of those thinking the Illuminati are the dark masters controlling us. The new material I've read this weekend has led me to question this, but I still firmly believe there is such a grouping, whether it's them or not.

And I retain my firm conviction that most of Icke's pronouncements are spot-on.

But I'm unconvinced by his bizarre belief that our evil rulers are shape-shifting, blood-drinking alien reptiles. That's just too crazy even for me! – Or is it?

Frigging hell – if there's just a slim chance he's also right about that, we should all be extremely concerned and very, very afraid.

No, sod that for a game of soldiers, let's go into denial instead. Phew, that's much better!

September 9 – I would say it's a question of distinguishing the angels from the devils in our strangely distorted Alice in Wonderland world. But that would be over-simplistic and saturated in vivid but misleading religious imagery.

Things are rarely that simple and clear-cut. We're all hybrids, carrying positive and negative energy currents within us constantly fighting for supremacy. Each of us can be good or bad, a force for healing or destruction.

I just think that those in positions of great influence in our cash-obsessed system have often become intoxicated by power and possessions and would do anything to have more of both, tightening their grip of control over the rest of us until it becomes brutally avaricious and iron-fisted.

Of course, some relatively virtuous souls do reach the dizzy heights without becoming too badly infected – but they're in the minority and our whole warped version of reality is run and controlled by the ruthlessly self-absorbed.

That's my view, anyway.

Turning to lighter matters, we often find that hearing certain songs can instantly flip our minds back to particular times, people and places.

One of These Nights by the Eagles is a case in point. I always associate it with the first time I ever heard it in the mid-1970s at a pub called the Coach and Horses in High Wycombe, Bucks. I was there with a mate called Steve Cooper.

It was while I was still living in Slough, three years before moving to Dorset, and I was spellbound by this great song which was new and fresh and different. I bought the album with the same name a few days later on vinyl and was blown away by this brilliant American group.

A year and a bit later I was at a heavy rock gig at Skindles Hotel, beside the banks of the Thames at Maidenhead. I can't remember who was playing – might have been Manfred Mann's Earth Band, Curved Air, Stray or Back Street Crawler (minus founder Paul Kossoff, who had died by then) – I saw them all there.

Anyway, the deejay playing rock records before the live show to get people in the mood put on a single I hadn't heard before. I was getting quite into it when he suddenly took it off the turntable and smashed it.

Shame, I thought, I was enjoying that.

"That was the Sex Pistols – what a load of crap," he snorted. Just goes to show how blinkered some people can get where music's concerned.

The record was Anarchy in the UK and that was my introduction to the Pistols, who I immediately liked because they played no-frills rock with attitude.

I had a similar experience in the mid-1990s when my deejay pal Steve put on a terrific single that was similarly fresh and exciting during one of his disco and quiz nights at the Bell pub, Pokesdown.

"Who's that?" I asked, intrigued. "Oasis – the song's called Live Forever," he replied.

I went out and got the album Definitely Maybe the following day. And loved it.

Then there were the first times I saw the Beatles, Bowie, Kate Bush, Jethro Tull, Frankie Goes to Hollywood and Culture Club on TV and the many rock'n'roll, chart, 1980s and 1990s dance and club songs that remind me of great times with my Pinecliff, White Horse, Palmerston, Home Guard and Bell pals.

Also, the first occasions I heard Alice Cooper, Supertramp and the Police, and that wonderful day at Blackbushe Aerodrome in 1978 with Bob Dylan, Eric Clapton, Joan Armatrading and Graham Parker and the Rumour.

Enjoying amazing live performances by the Who, Roy Orbison, the Undertones, Rory Gallagher, UB40, Def Leppard, Patti Smith, Yes, the Jam, Thin Lizzy and the Clash.

Superb sets from Motorhead, the Kinks, Alex Harvey, Iron Maiden, ELP, Hawkwind, Gillan, Frankie Valli and the Four Seasons, Status Quo, the Stranglers, Black Sabbath, Saxon, Wishbone Ash, UFO, Girlschool, the Specials, the Tygers of Pan

Tang, Slade, Curved Air, Judas Priest, Gary Numan, Chuck Berry and the Black Star Riders.

And Bill Wyman's excellent charity concert at Ringwood with Gary Brooker, Andy Fairweather-Low and the sublime, show-stealing Labi Siffre.

I remember all with great fondness and clarity, such was their impact on me.

And, of course, Stevie Wonder's I Just Called to Say I Love You – not one of his better tracks but it always reminds me of my ex-wife Joe as it was "our song."

Oh bum! – Just mentioning Jethro Tull caused me to break off from typing to check something. And it confirmed my worst fears.

Yes, I had indeed quite unforgivably omitted this tremendous group from my all-time top 30 list as presented in Persistent Illusions. That's almost as bad as missing Bob Dylan out of my summary of my top 20 favourite male performers.

Both deeply embarrassing errors show graphically how damned tough it is to compile such lists. To state the obvious, including Tull and Dylan would have meant dropping other outstanding bands and individuals.

I still love writing such rundowns though. You've might have noticed. Having said that, they're constantly subject to review and amendment.

But certain genius acts will always be at or near the top – whether I'm talking music stars, their albums, live sets, films, comedians, TV shows, books or their writers.

September 11 – A date to send icy shivers down the spine. I've lit a candle in remembrance of the victims of the insane carnage on that dreadful day 13 years ago.

So who's worse do you reckon? Those who take part in mass murder to ram home a twisted ideological point – or government ministers making declarations and decisions that cause widespread deaths and misery?

A racist bigot or a blinkered religious or political zealot?

A child abuser or a vicious mugger of old people?

A con artist always on the scam or a fraudulent cheat constantly fiddling expenses and dodging taxes?

A work-shy guy on benefits or a bloke in a job who frequently and deliberately cuts corners, endangering others?

A rapist or someone who regularly uses sickening violence?

A compulsive burglar or a person always stealing from family and friends?

A coward who flees danger, abandoning others to save his own skin – or a psycho who maims people for fun?

A soldier who deserts his post putting comrades at risk, or one who snaps under pressure and kills his sergeant-major?

Those with a penchant for illegal drugs – or heavy drinkers causing havoc?

A nasty sexist or someone who treats all people with respect but brutalises animals?

Think very carefully before you answer any of these questions. All of the above are odious and most of them, illegal.

But many folk have been guilty of at least one; some of two or more.

Our perception of the gravity of such crimes depends very much on our own personal mindset regarding ethics, values and priorities. Rampant hypocrisy also has a lot to do with it.

What I'm trying to do is illustrate how we can all be very selective and self-serving when we start talking about crime and punishment.

We all roundly condemn those resorting to some of these activities while condoning or turning a blind eye to others – possibly because they're a bit too close to home for comfort!

I've said it many times and I'll keep on doing so – we all do wrong and we all mess up, frequently, one way or another. Those who have done none of the above will be just as guilty of other misdemeanours or bad behaviour. Fact!

Legal systems must be in place to deal with offenders, especially where serious crime is concerned. But we must keep in mind that none of us is squeaky clean and we need to balance any person's faults and wrongdoings against their better qualities and virtuous acts benefiting others.

September 12 – Much-loved veteran actor Sir Donald Sinden has died at his home. He was 90.

He came to prominence in the 1950s and carved an impressive career in theatre, films, television and radio. He was equally at home playing straight roles and comedy and was highly regarded for his Shakespearean work.

One of my abiding memories of him was playing an antique dealer in the TV sitcom Never the Twain, co-starring Windsor Davies as his bitter rival. They were both superb and very funny.

I recently saw Sinden in an old episode of TV detective series Midsomer Murders, being repeated on a nostalgia channel. He was playing a pompous retired Army colonel with his usual skill and consummate ease.

I'm listening to some superlative reggae as I write this, courtesy of the quite splendid Steel Pulse. Earlier I played the equally brilliant Black Uhuru and yesterday I thoroughly enjoyed spinning CD albums by Aswad and the Specials.

I've been thinking more about the outrageous claim that the Beatles were part of some massive top-secret mind control experiment intended to brainwash the masses.

While I doubt this very much in their case – they were far too clever, free-thinking, irreverent, mischievous, warm, witty, funny and perceptive – I don't doubt that such experiments could be carried out on an unsuspecting public.

I believe that's especially true in this age of mass media, social networks, overnight sensations, shallow people, widespread spin and safe, bland, manufactured pop groups who never say a word that's meaningful or controversial and appear unable to utter anything of note, write songs or play instruments.

If you made the same allegation about a modern-day girl or boy band I would accept it as a possibility. Still unlikely, but a distinct possibility.

Of course, it's very true that the Beatles themselves started off as the biggest manufactured boy band of all time. But there was so much more to them and we quickly saw it as they proceeded to shake off the chains of convention.

They only went along with Brian Epstein's smart suits and discipline regime to begin with because they were wise enough to see this was the best way to get established.

But then they, and other like-minded pioneers, ushered in the 1960s explosion of new ideas that challenged and radically changed stuffy old establishment mindsets.

Yes, they used the system and arguably sold out – but they never, ever bought into it. They were far too shrewd and independent-minded for that.

Sadly, others who also reach the dizzy heights aren't as bright – so in their case brain control experiments are definitely on the cards. Got the time, Joey?

Let's face it; we have to take so much on trust these days. Controversy rages over what goes in our food and drinks with some claiming both are being dosed with mind-altering chemicals. Genetically modified produce and the fluoride put in water supplies are particular favourites mentioned in this debate.

There's also the huge, all-powerful pharmaceutical industry and the drugs people take into their bodies – prescription or otherwise. Are these also being meddled with?

Meanwhile, it seems our every move is being watched on CCTV cameras.

And micro-chipping pets – could this be the precursor of chipping humans at birth, putting them at the mercy of unscrupulous manipulators aiming to create a slave race?

To some all this will sound like crazy talk designed to scare us – so they'll just ignore anything that resembles even a slight diversion from straight, conventional reality.

And therein could lie the biggest danger of all – closed minds and voluntary ignorance. A manipulator's dream.

More and more citizens are coming to the conclusion that we're not being told the truth and some of these scenarios are actually within the realms of possibility.

We desperately and urgently need a new system based on honesty and fairness, where nothing is done without the full knowledge and consent of the people.

But who's going to deliver it? – certainly not the politicians in charge at the moment. This is why so many voters are turning to fast-growing minority parties in the hope they are more truthful and transparent.

September 13 – Two more famous people have kicked the bucket –actor John Bardon and politician the Reverend Ian Paisley.

Bardon, who was 75, is probably best known for playing mischievous pensioner Jim Branning in TV soap EastEnders.

Paisley, 88, was a former rabble-rousing firebrand Protestant leader who came to prominence as Northern Ireland's bitter and bloody civil war reached a high point in the second half of the 20th century.

He passionately opposed Roman Catholicism and homosexuality – but in later years he mellowed and became a key participant in the Good Friday agreement that finally brought peace to the province in 1998.

Both men will be missed but for vividly contrasting reasons.

In a more cheerful vein, I'd like to wish a very happy birthday to my friend Tina Mcauley.

September 14 – I've just watched an item on today's TV news about the government proposing new measures to protect the interests of crime victims. Good! – My own disgust at the way the system treated me after I was bashed up is well documented.

But hot on the heels of this welcome piece of information about a coalition policy I actually support, we had another bulletin in the same news broadcast revealing that PM David Cameron had very quickly got back to his usual belligerent, irritating self.

He said the beheading of a British aid worker in Syria, said to be the work of Islamic extremists, was an act of "pure evil."

No shit, Sherlock!

Anyone with an iota of decency or compassion would wholeheartedly agree, no matter what their cultural or religious standing. No doubt most peace-loving Muslims are equally sickened and appalled.

But, as usual with callous Cameron, it's the motive behind the comment that really infuriates.

The grisly butchering of the unfortunate aid worker has given him yet another reason to verbally bash Muslims and talk tough without making any attempt to find a peaceful solution to an ideological war that's fast getting out of hand.

In short, he's not helping at all; he's just making matters worse – again.

I saw a repulsive video on Facebook the other day that featured an American guy in full combat uniform wielding a rifle and crossbow and burning a copy of the Quran.

This right-wing nut, claiming to be a Christian, said Islam was supposed to be a peaceful religion but extremists were using it as an excuse to kill and maim innocents.

His aggressive hate-fuelled attitude was "okay, bring it on mother fuckers – we'll fight back hard and you'll never win."

Hardly a helpful or reasoned contribution to the debate, and the bitter irony of his words and actions clearly escaped this mentally unhinged moron.

The really shocking fact is that thousands of people all over the world had supported his video by pressing the "like" button – including a friend of mine.

And that had started a heated Facebook exchange between him (my friend) and another mutual mate incensed by his support for the video-maker.

Spitting out toxic venom like the American idiot, making violent threats and burning a so-called holy book or a national flag are always pretty effective ways of putting your point across.

A book is only paper and a flag is only cloth. It's the stark symbolism of the incendiary and provocative act that really fans the flames of division and conflict.

And violent crazies of all persuasions – Muslim, Christian, Jewish or whichever religion, from whatever cultural background – are just as guilty as each other in prolonging the killing, maiming and misery. And that's madness!

Violence is abhorrent and should only be used, if at all, in a minimal, restrained way as a last resort to defend ourselves or others. We should never strike first – attack.

And we should be a lot less prone to recklessly spew forth nasty, poisonous and inflammatory words and statements – even when provoked. All of us – me too.

Some of the angry and confrontational stuff I read on the Internet turns my stomach. But, obnoxious as I find these views and comments, I still passionately defend people's rights to hold and express them. It's called freedom of speech.

The pretty fruitless argument that flared up between my two friends on Facebook illustrates the point so very well. They each felt strongly about an issue and took up contradictory positions. Neither was going to budge, neither was going to win.

It vividly brought home to me the crux of the whole division and conflict problem.

Why the hell can't people with contrasting ideas, values and worldviews just agree to differ and respect each other's stances like mature grown-ups, not resort to childish petulance and retaliation that can so easily spiral out of control?

Because that way lies, resentment, friction, bitterness, violent clashes and in more extreme cases, frenzied bloodbaths. Am I wrong?

September 15 – Had a lovely evening in the Bell last night with mates including John Gaynor, Matt and Dani, Ben and Jenny and Sam Lowney.

Also there was DJ Darren Spence, a regular at the pub who recently won a nationwide karaoke competition and is off to Sweden soon to take part in the world finals. Well done Dazza and all the best for the big one.

His victory in the UK competition is more than good enough publicity for the dear old Bell. To do well in the world stakes would be amazing. Power to your elbow, pal!

Same date, a few hours later – Foreign ministers from around the world, including the USA and UK, have been meeting in Paris today to discuss the perceived growing threat of a group called Islamic State (IS).

The talks were arranged to agree a strategy to combat the group, said to control large parts of Iraq and Syria.

And they ended a short while ago with representatives of 30 countries pledging to help Iraq fight alleged hard line IS militants "by all means necessary".

A joint statement after today's talks said support would include "appropriate military assistance" – whatever that means.

The conference followed a whirlwind tour of the Middle East by US Secretary of State John Kerry.

Kerry, who attended the summit, has been drumming up support for a plan of action unveiled by President Barack Obama last week.

The beheading of British aid worker David Haines in Syria, said to be the work of IS militants, has added momentum to that plan, says the BBC.

A macabre video put on the Internet at the weekend showed men who claimed to be members of IS carrying out the savage and shocking act.

Opening the summit, French President Francois Hollande said the threat posed by IS militants needed a global response.

The CIA estimates that the group – formerly known as ISIS – has between 20,000 and 31,000 fighters in Iraq and Syria. It's seen to represent a major threat to world peace.

And it's said radicalised British Muslims have gone out to get involved in these bloody conflicts in the Middle-East.

I use words like "perceived", "alleged", apparently" and "seen to" because I don't know one way or the other and I certainly have no wish to add fuel to any fires.

You might be thinking "there he goes again – sitting on the fence as usual."

But I always advocate considering all sides in any argument – whether it's a minor spat between friends or a major issue with global implications.

I firmly advise impartiality and great caution in dealing with such emotionally-charged matters. And I'm talking to myself here as much as anyone else.

People – and nations – need protection from unhinged nutters and the followers they've brainwashed into supporting them.

But, when it comes to what we hear from the media, I say how on Earth can we be sure we're being told anything like the truth in this world of smoke and mirrors, spin and exaggeration?

Especially when time and time again those we rely on for vital information are exposed as having their own agendas, determined to twist and obscure the facts to suit their needs in a mad drive to push those agendas forward.

I despise brutal acts like David Haines' beheading and the murder of Lee Rigby – no matter who's responsible. Same with 911, the London Bombs or any other atrocity.

Any normal person with compassion and a conscience would.

But we're not dealing with normal people here, but the mentally unstable from all ideological sectors – whether they're hate-peddling street corner rabble rousers, narrow-minded trigger-happy meatheads or other deluded crazies using politics and religion as excuses to cause mayhem.

And when fiery rhetoric gives way to violent actions, the big question is how do we effectively respond to douse the flames, solve the problems and find a peaceful way forwards?

In other words, how do you negotiate with a sick mind?

We all need to be shielded from danger – but rapidly springing into combat mode just plays right into the nutters' hands, doesn't help, and in fact makes matters much worse and us no better than them.

One way to stop the strife and contain the threats would be to listen to grievances and use common sense and compassion in locating the sources and working with great care and diplomacy to remove them.

Unfairness, greed, jealousy and prejudice are frequently among the causes.

But far too often politicians just talk tough and send in the troops and bombers, intensifying the situation and making our world an even more hazardous place. Makes you wonder why, don't it?

The answer could support my view that there's a sinister, shadowy network of twisted individuals in positions of great power and influence with a vested interest in keeping us edgy, fearful and fighting each other as a means to retain its tight control while keeping a safe distance from the resultant deaths and destruction.

Yep – we're back there again. Wild conspiracy theory? Maybe, but I think not. And I'm getting more and more convinced I'm right. My only question now is what this network's name is – if it even has one.

Let's get one thing straight here – I'm no apologist for radical Islam or the sickening violence perpetrated and perpetuated in its name.

But neither will I ever tacitly accept the hard-edged views or lethal actions of nut jobs who claim to be Christians. I detest savagely aggressive extremism full stop.

If mass mind control projects do exist, brainwashed, blinkered boneheads of all persuasions are prime candidates. Politics and religion are ideal vehicles for such cynical manipulation.

****

CHAPTER THREE – UNSETTLING TIMES

September 16 – Oh dear, oh dear – Uncle Sam's done it again. Sent in the bombers, that is.

America has carried out an air strike against Islamic State (IS) militants in Iraq under a new strategy to defeat the group. Others will no doubt follow.

The US military said yesterday's strike had destroyed an IS fighting position south-west of Baghdad that had been firing on Iraqi forces.

So this is what constitutes "appropriate military assistance". Might have known!

So Barack Obama has joined Jimmy Carter and Bill Clinton in being a Democrat president ordering airborne attacks on targets in the Middle East.

That's as contradictory as a Labour government here spearheading invasions of Afghanistan and Iraq in the early years of this century. It seems to belie the political party's core principles.

Sure, aggressors using extreme violence, oppression and intimidation need to be stopped in their tracks. People who can't defend themselves have to be protected.

That's stating the obvious. But my big question is who should do it – citizens within those countries, neighbouring states or others thousands of miles away who wouldn't be involved unless they chose to be?

And you could argue that Iraq's problems and instability were partly caused by the 2003 US/UK invasion to oust Saddam Hussein.

Like IS, he was seen as an evil force causing deaths and misery. We were told he similarly had to be neutralised before he did more harm.

And we all know we can rely on governments and the media to tell us the truth, don't we? Yeah, right!

I'm listening to Kate Bush's terrific double album Aerial as I type away here.

You may consider my choice of background music puzzling and more than a tad incongruous in this context. And certainly War Pigs by Black Sabbath would seem a lot more appropriate, given my subject matter.

But playing Kate's CD provides a vivid and rather nice contrast – reminding me that there is still harmony and beauty in this world as well as violent discord and gut-wrenching ugliness.

And when it comes to war and military matters, Kate and I seem to share a peace-loving, pacifist view. Check out the words to Army Dreamers, the third single released from her 1980 album Never for Ever.

Well, there's two days left before Scots make their big decision – whether to stay in the United Kingdom or go for independence, splitting it asunder. Exciting but quite unsettling times for us all!

September 17 – Most afternoons I watch old episodes of the Jeremy Kyle Show on ITV Two. Most of my nearest and dearest hate him with a passion and so do I – but for some strange reason I find his show perversely compulsive viewing.

I've mentioned my own deep resentment for this despicable man before. He's grossly opinionated, amazingly big-headed, totally self-absorbed and patently ignorant.

He deliberately winds people up and when they bite back he acts like he owns the whole of Manchester (where it's filmed) as he tells them angrily to "get off my stage" and "get out of my building." What an egocentric pillock!

I find his frequent references to being an old man both ridiculous and very annoying. Get a grip you dolt; you're only 49 for goodness' sake!

What makes it even more infuriating is the fact that at the same time he seems to think anyone over 60 shouldn't have a life or anything resembling fun or excitement but meekly melt into the background, quietly knitting or pottering around allotments.

His studio audience laps up his brutally biased, ill-informed tirades and his patronising remarks. It makes me wonder where the heck they get such unthinking, compliant fools.

And his guests are even worse, displaying incredible levels of stupidity, irrational spite and crazed aggression.

One guy on yesterday's repeated show really got on my wick. Accused of having an affair, he swore on his daughter's life that he hadn't.

A lie detector told us otherwise, but even if he had been telling the truth, using his own child's welfare so recklessly and cynically was just plain evil in my book.

I hate it when people do that. If you want to swear something on you own life, it's still very wrong but it's your personal existence being trusted to fickle fortune, no-one else's. So it's your lookout and your funeral if the high-stakes gamble backfires.

It's never a good idea to tempt fate – especially when you do it with another person's wellbeing. To swear on a loved one's life rather than your own is to be a total git and an absolute coward. And if it's a youngster's, that really is the lowest of the low.

Today's telly news included a story about the murders of two British tourists in Thailand. Two other Brits are being questioned.

The dear old BBC also spoke in dramatic terms about it being the last day before the historic Scottish referendum. It's still too close to call, with the anti-independence, pro-UK lobby a whisker's breadth ahead.

But even if the Scots vote for independence, nothing much will change immediately as there will be an 18-month transition period while the details are sorted out.

Today also saw the release of the monthly unemployment figures, showing another drop in the jobless total. Okay guys, if you say so (yawn).

But the dear old Beeb did point out that, despite these apparently good tidings, pay rises weren't keeping pace with inflation and millions were still struggling to cope financially – a lot worse off than they were before austerity measures kicked in.

Too right – and what about those left high and dry, expected to pay their bills with thin air, lacking proper , secure paid work but now prevented from claiming benefits?

Ask them what they feel about the latest figures and the government's smug claims that its hard line policies are working.

I've been reading a fair bit on the Internet about The Quran, the Bible and what they say about using violence against your enemies. It's an eye-opener, I can tell you!

Of course, we have to bear in mind that all information can be twisted to suit someone's agenda – whether it's in the original texts, their translations or the way they're interpreted through media such as the worldwide web.

Preachers have for centuries been extremely selective in which bits of their holy books they use and which they ignore because they contradict what they're trying to say from their pulpits or street corner soap boxes.

Now we get the same bias and out-of-context repetitions on a global scale, increasing confusion and misunderstanding a thousand fold.

Y'shua (Jesus) is quoted many times advocating peace and tolerance. Love your enemies; turn the other cheek and all that. But that's the New Testament.

The Old Testament, by contrast, is full of fire and brimstone quotes and tales of extreme violence being used in God's name.

The Quran accepts Jesus as a prophet and also advocates tolerance and living in harmony – but at the same time contains similarly inflammatory language promoting murder and brutality in Allah's cause.

It's a mind-bender, that's for sure. No wonder believers have sharply clashing opinions, leading to disagreements, confrontation and bitter fighting.

And no wonder so many are atheists, swerving any kind of religious indoctrination.

There are similarly heated debates about what the holy books say about other vital issues such as homosexuality.

Muhammad and The Quran appear to roundly condemn it in the most unequivocal terms possible. And yet there are gay Muslims.

Y'shua says nothing definitive on the subject at all – but Saul (Paul) comes out strongly against it in his New Testament letters to Christian communities. And various sections of the Old Testament are dead against it with warnings of transgressors burning in hell.

So, it seems, while the New Testament can be interpreted according to whether you're a follower of Y'shua or Saul, the Old Testament and Quran both reek with hatred, intolerance and calls for violent retribution.

And, of course, Jews use the Old Testament in preference to the new, refusing to accept Jesus as a prophet, let alone a messiah.

One of Christianity's hugest ironies is the fact that many who purport to follow its peace-loving founder use extreme violence in his name. That's just sick and insane.

The religious wars and ideological disputes that plague our modern world seem to be the result of people continuing to use millennia-old mindsets in a 21st century setting.

This is precisely why knee-jerk reactions and fighting fire with fire will never work in sorting out problems and bringing peace.

The conflict has raged through centuries and its roots date back eons. Over time, new political, religious or cultural ideas have constantly come into play as ideologies have split and split again.

Social and technological advances, the discovery of precious metals and the creation of money led to a host of -isms including capitalism, communism and humanism.

Sadly the one that's always been around is fascism – although it wasn't called that until the 20th century. It's still very much with us – and worryingly on the rise again.

I see truth in all belief systems but think each one's been perverted to suit people's own paradigms, dreams and personal agendas – whether they've been revered saints, visionaries, prophets or so-called ordinary citizens of our troubled planet.

I feel strongly that wisdom comes from knowledge – and that's the real key to enlightenment. Spirituality should triumph over rigidly fixed ideas and age-old dogmas that hold us back and prevent us learning and growing as individuals.

Our minds should remain flexible, open to challenging revelations and evolving truth. Tragically, far too many people – me included – let familiar but erroneous mindsets and ego get in the way of real progress and proper evolution.

The more I learn, the more I change my perceptions of the range of possibilities. I no longer think the same as I did when I started the first volume of *Sunshine and Ice*.

Some might consider this a bad thing, showing I'm flaky and easily led. I prefer to call it open-minded. I despair at those who cling desperately to old, familiar ideas and belief systems, refusing point blank to even consider other concepts and explanations.

They probably find great comfort in this and are terrified that doubt will creep in, destroying their cosy paradigm and leaving them vulnerable and unsure. But I think they're denying themselves a chance to grow in wisdom and spiritual maturity.

Not that I'm spiritually mature – far from it. I'm still very wobbly on my feet. The difference is I know it.

You'll notice I refer to Y'shua and Saul. Y'shua was the Hebrew name of the man more commonly called Jesus Christ. Jesus is the Latin version and is still a very popular first name in Latin countries such as Spain and Mexico. Christ is not a surname but means anointed one, or messiah.

Saul, born in Tarsus, Turkey, is far better known as Paul, his Roman citizen name. He's said to have been converted to Christianity on the road to Damascus, Syria.

And all the 12 apostles' names were changed as the religion spread. They obviously weren't really called John, James, Thomas, Matthew, Andrew or Simon Peter – these are just our Westernised versions of their Hebrew monikers.

It's claimed that Y'shua never intended to form a new religion and his aim was to transform the Jewish faith he was proud to belong to.

Incidentally, it's also said that Christianity as we know it today owes a lot more to Saul than Y'shua.

And it's true that priests and church ministers spend at least as much of their time in pulpits quoting his words as they do those of the religion's accidental founder.

Chucked out of the embryonic church formed among Y'shua's family and closest friends after heated theological disagreements, Saul flounced off and started up his own rival faith, it's alleged.

This is the one that took off big time as it was spread across the globe by the all-powerful Roman Empire before its demise. And it's what we now call Christianity.

Although largely eclipsed, the original spiritual community formed by Y'shua's nearest and dearest actually survived – and pockets of it can still be found even today in the Holy Land. It preaches a purer form of his message, it's claimed.

Women are also apparently a lot more accepted in its top positions than they have been for millennia in Saul's now-global enterprise.

This ties in with the idea that Mary Magdalene and the sisters Martha and Mary (Lazarus's siblings) were at least as important to Y'shua himself as any of his male disciples – maybe even more so.

September 18 – Well, it's arrived at last, decision day for Scotland. Four million citizens are going to the polls to choose between staying in the United Kingdom and leaving it to become an independent country.

Scotland has given so much to the world in both human terms and natural resources. Some of the greatest creative, inventive, astute and philosophical minds have come from there.

The same is true of England, Wales and Ireland of course. Together or apart, we can still all give so much more.

No matter which way the referendum goes, we should remain bosom buddies, blood brothers and sisters. There's no need for friction, no reason to fall out.

Greatness is evident both sides of the border. Real treasures are to be found, both in the Scottish land itself and the qualities and talents of its people.

To revive some earlier imagery in a totally different context, I suppose you could say they have the diamonds and we have the gold.

Scotland's fate was top of the news on TV this morning. Another item concerned a Chinese online shopping company set to become the biggest stock market sensation of all time. It's called Alibaba – doesn't sound very Chinese to me, more Iraqi.

We also heard that reports of Islamic State's rise and a child abuse scandal in Rotherham had helped spark an extreme right-wing backlash in our fair land.

Like we didn't see that coming – and like it wasn't part of the evil game plan!

Speaking of Iraq and Islamic State dovetails into my next subject.

With nothing I particularly wanted to watch on telly last night, I ended up viewing once again my DVD of Michael Moore's controversial documentary film *Fahrenheit 911*. And I found it strikingly topical.

Many will say this movie is outrageously biased and conspiracy theory in overdrive.

Maybe, but I welcome any media project that sticks up for the unfortunate victims of the merciless global military-industrial machine and the ruthless sick nuts who run it.

The film begins with Republican candidate George W Bush's highly-disputed victory in the 2000 American presidential election that many say his Democrat rival Al Gore actually won but the figures were later fixed in Bush's favour.

It then relates the gruesome nightmare and heartbreaking tragedy of 911, followed by the horror and hatred involved in the 2003 invasion of Iraq.

Watching it again, six days after the anniversary of 911, made it topical enough. But the shocking scenes of the Iraq debacle posed a question – could this be one of the reasons for the later rise of Islamic State? I would suggest the answer's yes.

Moore told us that Iraq was no threat to the United States, unlike Osama bin Laden, al-Qaeda and the Saudis named as the perpetrators of 911. In fact, bin Laden had been identified as involved in earlier terrorist attacks and was already on at least one FBI most wanted list.

So it's hardly surprising the formerly peace-loving ordinary people of Iraq turned so violently against the invaders bombing and killing them. In their shoes, wouldn't you?

Yes, by all accounts Saddam Hussein was a monster who needed taming – but innocent Iraqis were paying a very high price for America's obsessive hatred of him.

I've just had a thought – as our leaders bang on about being greener and saving the planet, how environment-friendly is a Cruise missile or helicopter gunship?

Anyway, back to Moore's movie, he suggests that lucrative business links with super rich Saudi Arabians meant no-one was going to upset them, even though most of the people named in the plane hijacker list put out after 911 were from that country.

So was the bin Laden family, with whom the Bushes had shared commercial interests.

Moore comes out firmly in favour of the poor Iraqis who bore the brunt of Western aggression – he says partly because their country was rich in oil reserves. But he also passionately supports poor young Americans so cruelly conned into waging war.

He names massive companies such as the Carlyle Group, Halliburton and Enron as major players in the whole sordid affair – providing the weapons for attack and the materials to rebuild the country afterwards, making millions of dollars in the process.

And he notes that it's America's poverty-stricken communities that often supply the youngsters willing to fight the politicians' battles for them – while thinking they're serving their country, protecting it from harm. It's rarely the kids of wealthy business folk or the politicians who work with them to retain control and amass more cash.

In other words, it's always those at the bottom of the pile who are the first to put their lives on the line for a system that's done them no favours at all, he asserts.

Interestingly, David Icke mentions the same companies in his books about the callous network of despicable individuals he says are determined to run the world for their own benefit, oblivious to any pain, suffering or multiple deaths they might cause.

But Icke does take issue with Moore on certain aspects, even though they seem to agree on an awful lot.

Me? – I think they're both right far too often for comfort.

And, as Moore correctly points out, if you scare people witless, stir them up then propel them into blood-soaked confrontations, you're going to get a horror show.

I would add that it will run and run with no winners until someone has the guts and vision to reject ceaseless violent attack and retaliation and labour tirelessly to bring peace. But there's slim chance of that with the self-serving creeps currently in charge.

September 19 – Happy ruby birthday Cass Kelly, 40 today. I met her through our mutual friend Sam Excell when she came over to visit from her native Northern Ireland. She lives there with her man Howard.

Poor Cass has had major health worries of late. I hope she has a fab day and I wish her all the best for the future.

Back home now, Cass has also lived in both England and Scotland, which yesterday voted by 55 per cent to 45 per cent to stay in the United Kingdom.

Only four of the 32 polling areas voted yes to independence – but they included Glasgow, the biggest. And yet the Scots sent a crystal clear message to the Whitehall politicians – heed the people's views, concerns and desires instead of stubbornly enforcing your own agendas, ignoring voters' wishes.

It's a message they'd do well to act upon, for I've no doubt citizens in England, Wales and Northern Ireland feel the same. This was a massive wake-up call for the smug elite running our country.

And talking of elites, I've been looking further into the whole Illuminati issue. The popular view is that this is the name of the privileged, rather sinister few in positions of great power controlling and manipulating reality as we know it for their own selfish, perverted purposes.

But that's wrong, says the guy claiming to be one of its leaders. The Old World Order dating back millennia is the privileged elite and his group wants the direct opposite – power passed to the people in a radical New World Order benefiting all.

It wishes to replace aggressive capitalism with a more socialist-minded meritocracy, with citizens reaching top positions based on their skills and intelligence, not wealth and privileged backgrounds, he claims.

At first glance these seem like excellent and altruistic aims. And his opinions on religion and the drawbacks of the major faiths had also struck a chord in me.

But reading further on the pro-Illuminati website yesterday, alarm bells started to ring.

To explain, there's much more there than I originally thought. Until then I'd only skimmed the surface, viewing the top bit containing the interview with the anonymous feller and a few back-up pages, incorrectly believing that was it.

But I discovered more pages when I looked up the site again yesterday – and realized that I was still only about half-way through.

The first worrying revelation was that democracy as we know it would also go out with hard line capitalism. As a democrat, this made me more than a bit nervous.

The second thing to jar was the realization that nowhere did there seem to be mention of the less bright and mentally challenged. By implication, they would sink to the bottom of the pile.

This smacked of Darwin's rather cold and harsh survival of the fittest theory beloved of the far right. And it made me ask – why should kind, decent human beings be punished just because they're not blessed with high IQs?

This seemed wrong to me – seriously so.

I was also far from happy with the great importance attributed to mathematical formulas and calculations, said to be the building blocks of our universe and a source of great divinity.

There is no doubt at least some truth in this and I do accept numerology and sacred geometry as quite possibly very powerful influences. But giving this much prominence to stark mathematics seemed a bit clinical and soulless to me.

And with the Illuminati's planned outlawing of all inheritance payments, I would have stayed struggling on benefits without the cash to get my books published.

Putting ceilings on the amount of wealth that can be passed on after death is certainly a good idea. But a complete ban would hit lower-income people the worst – bad!

I remain unsure if the Illuminati are actually the villains they're portrayed as. The parts of the website I viewed initially made me wonder if I'd previously got it wrong in seeing them that way. But the bits I read yesterday planted new seeds of doubt.

I'm gonna keep on looking up this site and others while leaving my mind wide open to the full range of possibilities.

You might have gathered that I find all this stuff pretty flipping absorbing.

Incidentally, I've also recently been looking into George Galloway's Respect Party and its stated aims, many of which I applaud.

But I still maintain that the Greens have the best policies, balancing care for our planet and the other species we share it with while working from within to transform the democratic process, forging fairer, more compassionate communities and placing the power back in the hands of the people at a more localized level.

This applies both in the home nations and Europe. Rather than quitting the EU, which could have serious repercussions for us all, they say we should work together with other Greens from neighbouring nations to change it to the same ends. I agree.

September 20 – Fantastic! Phil and Emily came to see me earlier today with little Chloe. (Lucas was on holiday with his mum and Harvey was with Em's parents.)

Chloe is a real character and bright as a button. And she can now say "granddad" which is so cool. Happy, happy Martin.

****

CHAPTER FOUR – VAMPIRES

September 21 – Do you reckon there are vampires among us? I do – and would argue that they're as big a problem in the modern world as they've ever been.

I'm not talking about the blood-drinking kind from horror movies – although there probably are some deranged loons partial to a tipple of the old rhesus positive who might even take part in bizarre and chilling human sacrifices.

The vampires I'm on about are those overbearing individuals who suck you dry of energy and drain you mentally and emotionally, leaving you stunned and wrecked.

And there are far too many of them around, always have been. They're the kings and queens of manipulation, totally self-obsessed and always wanting to be the centre of attention, constantly getting others to dance to their tunes.

Most of us have at least one of these people in our lives. Sometimes we quite desperately need a rest from them – time to relax and recuperate.

One feller who definitely wasn't a social vampire was my Uncle Jack, Dad's brother, who died two years ago today. He was lovely man, so kind, thoughtful and funny. I've lit a candle for him.

September 22 – Had a fab evening at the Bell last night with mates – John Palmer, John Gaynor, Matt Brandt, Dani Knight, Bev Jones, Tim Robbins, Becky Browning, Ben Avill, guv'nors Laura Williams and Mark Evans and barmaid Tamzin Lee, plus karaoke and disco supremo DJ Ross Maslin playing super-cool old school sounds.

I've just taken a lovely walk down to Southbourne cliff top in the bright sunshine. I love living this close to the seafront.

Oh Gawd – Basher Blair's back in the building!

Former Labour PM Tony B – the man who unforgivably led our country to invade Afghanistan and Iraq – has now made similarly warlike comments about Islamic State.

He said sending in combat troops to fight IS militants on the ground should not be ruled out.

Way to go Tone – that'll bring peace to the Middle East. Prat!

So once again Labour and the Tories are singing from the same battle hymn sheet over aggressive foreign policies. No wonder there's been a rise in radical Islam.

Let's face it; you can't really distinguish between the two main parties these days over anything of importance – be it the Middle East, the European super-state, caring for the environment or axing people's benefits at home.

The Liberal Democrats are just the same now after tasting power and ditching their former persona of the party of peace and common sense to become toothless Tory lapdogs.

Labour leader Ed Miliband and his shadow cabinet MPs will be trying very hard at their party's conference in Manchester this week to convince their own faithful and us that they are a radical alternative and would look after us better in government.

Funny innit? – that's what both Labour and the Lib Debs previously said in opposition – only to show they were just as dreadful as the Tories on actually getting into power.

September 23 – Hello again. I'm bonkers, what's your excuse? Happy autumn equinox, girls and boys.

America has launched air strikes against Islamic State in Syria as the Middle East conflict escalates. Our government supports this action.

Labour MPs who previously opposed military intervention in the troubled country are also now backing the idea, claiming the situation out there has changed.

The Tories similarly meekly supported Labour's invasions of Afghanistan in 2001 and Iraq in 2003 – when they also had a golden opportunity to stand up for us, the people, by justifiably ripping into the government's mad and dangerous war plans.

Back then, the Lib Dems were the ones raising objections and promoting peace. Not any more – not now they're in the coalition government. It makes me so angry!

Why, oh why do our politicians insist on sounding off and getting embroiled in tribal conflicts on foreign soil – making us a prime target for enraged and radicalised nutters in the process?

I'm all for defending ourselves, our neighbours and allies against aggressors posing genuine threats. But all this goes way beyond that. It's insane!

Half a million more refugees are fleeing strife-torn Syria, pushing the total to over three million since the latest trouble kicked off there in 2011.

And more than 100,000 men, women and children have been killed since a crackdown on peaceful protests sparked the savage civil war in March of that year.

This is the tragic and deplorable human cost of such violent conflicts.

Apparently, five neighbouring Arab nations are backing America's actions. Why couldn't these countries have joined forces to help the oppressed Syrian and Iraqi residents and refugees while defending their own populations from any IS threats?

Why is the US involved at all? – And why are we leaping on its coat-tail yet again?

Am I being terribly naïve here? Bitter, millennia-old ideological power struggles, combined with existing lucrative oil reserves, have nothing to do with it, have they?

And there's absolutely no chance of personal fortunes being made by selling arms to whomever wants to buy, waging war on lands then rebuilding them, is there?

You might be wondering what's happened to al-Qaeda in all of this. We're not hearing much nowadays about the one-time big bad wolf said to be threatening world peace. Well, apparently Islamic State is an off-shoot. So now we know (it seems).

My home town of Slough is also in the news for the wrong reason. Police are investigating after two people were killed in suspicious circumstances, hit by a train at the local station.

September 25 – Following on from Basher Blair's armchair warrior comments the other day, we now have Prime Minister David Cameron stoking the fires of hatred.

He was on the TV news this morning saying that Britain was poised to "play its part" in fighting Islamic State, which he called an "evil against which the whole world must unite."

His comment comes as Parliament prepares to be recalled tomorrow to discuss a possible British involvement in air strikes on IS in Iraq.

A yes vote could see RAF planes joining the US, France and a number of Arab states in bombarding IS positions as early as this weekend. Oh bloody hell!

Cameron's phrasing of his inflammatory remark is both interesting and very alarming. To say Britain's ready to "play its part" carries the crystal clear implication that we have a military role to fulfil – and if we don't we're being remiss, letting others down.

This is dangerous talk indeed. We most certainly should be playing a part alright – providing humanitarian aid and practical assistance to unfortunate residents and refugees whose lives have been destroyed by blood-crazed lunatics.

But beyond that, it's a far from straightforward matter deciding whether we should involve ourselves in violent flare-ups thousands of miles away.

I would suggest the answer's an emphatic no – unless there are exceptional circumstances posing a genuine threat to us here on our own soil.

Otherwise, talking tough and sending in the bombers and troops just radicalizes more Muslims both abroad and in the UK, not helping but raising the stakes even higher.

In August 2013, I wrote that I was relieved that the Commons had voted against Cameron's proposal to launch similar air strikes against President Assad in Syria.

But I predicted that more pressure would be brought to bear to reverse this decision against military intervention.

Okay, tomorrow's vote is about Iraq – but it's a neighbouring country also being ripped apart by violent ideological conflict between IS and its opponents.

And if our MPs vote yes – as seems likely – how long will it be before we attack Syria as well? Only a matter of time, I'd suggest – quite possibly days. That was the original plan, after all.

Things are bad enough already for the brutalized and traumatized Iraqi and Syrian people. The last thing they need now is us launching missiles at their land and homes or tightly-wound soldiers marching into their towns and villages shooting everything that moves.

We're told the request for military intervention has come from Iraq. But who in Iraq? Presumably the government – which since Saddam's deposition has been in the West's pocket – asking us to assist in sorting out a mess we helped create, or at least aggravated.

And there's nothing to say air strikes or ground troops are the answer. Providing practical help and support for moderate Muslims opposing IS might be.

This whole issue perfectly illustrates my point about there being no real difference between the Conservatives and Labour over most matters of the greatest importance.

Politically and spiritually, Cameron and Blair are Thatcher's children. So are Osborne and Clegg for that matter – in Clegg's case, proven by his actions more than his words.

And speaking of words, the deliberate phrasing of Cameron's comment today is typical of how language is manipulated by our politicians and media folk to try to make us think in a certain way.

Another item on today's telly news further proved the point so well. It was updating us on the story of 14-year-old Alice Gross, missing since August 28 when she was last seen near the Grand Union Canal in west London.

It was said that as concern grew about her welfare, bids to find her represented the largest Metropolitan Police search operation since the 7/7 bombings in 2005.

Why on Earth describe it in these terms? The London Bombs terrorist attack is hardly comparable to the plight of a missing schoolgirl. The linking of the two would seem bizarre if it weren't for the inclusion of the deepening Iraq crisis on the same news.

The apparently out of place reference to 7/7, coming within minutes of the reporting of Cameron's Iraq statement, leads us to make a connection between IS and the London Bombs – just as intended.

Pure coincidence? – I think not. A cynical and sinister attempt to get us to support the game plan? Almost certainly.

While the BBC was so admirably helping the government to mess with our heads, the morning newspapers showed themselves as ridiculous as ever.

As our political leaders prepare to plunge us into yet another war – making further terrorist attacks on home soil pretty much inevitable – the tabloids led with the story of Jason Orange leaving Take That.

This is no doubt a very big deal for the pop group's fans, but in the great scheme of things it's hardly that important.

That's right Fleet Street – never mind the real issues, focus on the comparatively trivial while the world burns. Divert our attention with superficial showbiz stuff.

Until it really kicks off for us in Iraq and Syria, at which point you'll no doubt weigh in with your usual crass sensationalist drivel totally lacking any depth, intelligent comment, reasoned argument, balanced reporting or the slightest trace of sensitivity.

When you're not stirring it in other ways, that is – bashing Muslims, Eastern Europeans and benefit claimants in our own country.

Hate-laced comments annoy me intensely, whether they come in outrageously biased newspaper stories, politicians' warmongering statements, street corner preachers' extremist babblings or gun-toting crazies' Facebook video rants.

It's high time we had a lot more tolerance, acceptance and harmony, agreeing to differ and respecting others' views, even if we find them irrational, extreme or even obnoxious. Isn't it?

Turning from untrustworthy politicians and news folk to another of my bugbears, I saw a TV advert yesterday that really irritated me. Can't recall the product – not interested, doesn't matter – but once again I was appalled by the behaviour on display.

It shows a guy in the bathroom about to brush his teeth when he drops his blue toothbrush down the loo. He fishes it out then swaps it for a pink toothbrush that he then uses instead, putting his blue one in a tumbler the pink one had been in and the pink one in his own tumbler standing beside it.

Some will say lighten up, it's only a commercial – a bit of fun, not to be taken too seriously. But this advert is shown during the day when impressionable kids will be watching, going away with the idea it's okay to be that selfish, uncaring and devious.

Of course, if that happened in real life the owner of the pink toothbrush, presumably the man's partner, might well notice it's it the wrong tumbler – unless they were half-asleep or otherwise distracted, a distinct possibility.

But children wouldn't appreciate such subtleties – they would just see the guy doing what he did and think it's acceptable when it most certainly isn't.

A lot more care and thought should be exercised before putting commercials on TV.

They should be morally sound as well as entertaining – use wit and humour by all means but always show good behaviour being rewarded and those displaying bad traits getting their come-uppance.

Okay, sadly that doesn't always accurately reflect real life but surely we must all aspire to such ideals, even in something as trivial as a TV advert, for it will be seen by millions and could especially influence children if put out when they'd be watching.

I think commercials should be given age classifications like TV programmes or cinema films – and those with more adult content shouldn't be shown in the daytime.

The morally dubious or potentially offensive should be broadcast later – or not at all.

September 26 – I've got the big Iraq debate on telly as I type this. It's both absolutely crucial and very intriguing.

Cameron's basically saying he wants to rid the world of ISIL's "butchers and psychopaths" by any mean necessary. Miliband backs air strikes but advises caution, adding that most Muslims abhor the policies and acts of hard line ISIL extremists.

Anxious Green MP Caroline Lucas is the anti-violence voice of trepidation and reason – no surprise there – and even good old Tory grandee Ken Clarke reckons we've made mistakes in the Middle East that have intensified its problems. Well said, sir!

The reference to ISIL threw me a bit. To explain, it stands for the Islamic State of Iraq and Levant. The same organisation is often called ISIS, the Islamic State of Iraq and Syria, or more commonly simply IS, Islamic State.

Whichever handle you use, Britain and the West see it as a brutally-enforced rogue state, not representing the people of any of these territories.

The Commons debate on sending in the bombers rumbles on. But it's lunch time now so I need to stop typing and have a bite to eat.

September 27 – Didn't get a chance to resume my ramblings yesterday so here's the latest on the air strikes issue. The Commons predictably voted in favour of sending British war planes to bomb IS strongholds in Iraq, starting today or tomorrow.

The motion was passed by a massive majority, 524 to 43. Those voting against included the Greens' Caroline Lucas, the Respect Party's George Galloway, Labour's Kate Hoey, Dennis Skinner and Diane Abbott and Tory rebel John Baron.

In all, 23 Labour MPs, six Conservatives and one sole Liberal Democrat said no. At least some Parliamentary representatives still have consciences and common sense.

Six RAF Tornadoes stationed in Cyprus will initially be involved in the air strikes. But you can bet your bottom dollar more UK military action will follow.

And no doubt Syria will be next on the hit list, possibly very soon, and the deployment of ground troops seems inevitable with Cameron warning there's no quick-fix solution and our brave service folk could be out there for years.

We're told that a further vote in the Commons would be needed before similar strikes were launched against IS in Syria (officially, at least). But again I see a yes vote as pretty much a foregone conclusion – and I fear it's not that far away.

Brilliant! – So we're involved in yet another costly and open-ended military exercise on far-flung foreign soil that will only increase the likelihood of terrorist atrocities at home as more and more Muslims here become enraged, radicalised and turn violent.

Smart move guys. You assholes!

(Security services here have already raised the level of terrorist attack threat from substantial to severe – on August 29.)

Incidentally, I'm curious to know how the people would have voted had a national referendum been held on the crucial issue of our taking such drastic military action.

That would have been very interesting indeed. Okay, I accept that it would have taken months of planning and preparation and time is often of the essence in dealing with rapidly-unfolding developments at home and abroad.

I'm just saying that during our last general election, I doubt very much if citizens realized the guys they were voting for would lead us into yet another war with the increased domestic danger that implies.

September 28 – We're told that RAF war planes yesterday started making sorties over Iraqi land following Friday's Commons vote.

What a deliberately quaint way of describing a pretty damned aggressive act in order to downplay its impact!

The aircraft did not engage in any combat action – just took a look to send a message to the IS that we're watching them, said this morning's BBC news.

But America is continuing its air strikes in Iraq and Syria. I have little doubt it won't be long before we join them.

Cameron is keen to point out that it's not just America and us involved.

We're told that France and the Netherlands have already voted to launch similar air strikes in Iraq; Australia is behind the move, and neighbouring territories.

Saudi Arabia, Qatar, Jordan, Bahrain and the United Arab Emirates are all part of an alliance of more than 40 nations backing the plan.

My my – someone's been busy twisting arms, scaring people witless and drumming up support, haven't they?

Still doesn't make the warmongering action right though, does it?

An unspecified number of people have already died thanks to the US air strikes. More casualties are inevitable as the crisis escalates.

Citizens have also died here in the UK as a direct result of the government's austerity measures. Jobs have been lost, people impoverished and the NHS is under threat.

Yet we can always find the cash to wage wars. It's bloody obscene!

And believe it or not, Cameron's just been on the BBC news threatening even more benefit cuts if the Tories get back into power at next year's general election.

The frigging brass neck of the man!

He seems to have conveniently forgotten that he and his Conservative chums are only in power at all thanks to Nick Clegg and the Liberal Democrats.

If the nation had wanted a Tory government last time around people would have voted for one by a clear majority. But they didn't. Neither did they want Brown's tired old Labour continuing with its increasingly right-wing but muddled agenda.

The good news is that our peace-loving, compassionate Prime Minister, really in tune with his people's wishes (yeah, right!) isn't going to have it all his own way.

As the Conservatives gather for their party conference in Birmingham, we hear that two more members have left the ranks – one the centre of what's been described as a minor sex scandal involving lewd photographs.

It's the other one that I find a lot more interesting – a guy with the surname Reckless has defected to UKIP. Yeah I know – I'm saying no more.

Cameron should watch his back here. More defections to UKIP and more allegations of sleaze could start an unstoppable snowball of adverse publicity that would scupper his bid to return to power next May

He's already on very thin ice after the Scottish independence vote – and his position would have been untenable had it gone the other way.

If the Middle East situation worsens or we have another terrorist attack here – both highly likely in light of his own pronouncements and actions – he would almost certainly have to go.

It's no secret that I think his departure would be great news for our battered country. But I'm furious and deeply saddened that he's already caused so much devastation.

And I do wonder what the alternative would be – probably a right-leaning, equally out of touch Labour crew back in the driving seat, breaking promises, making the same mistakes and resembling a pseudo-Tory administration with a few minor differences.

Depressing, innit?

September 29 – Happy 40th birthday to my mate and former work colleague Lorna Lane. Hope she has a great one.

On the news, Barack O'Bomber continues with his air strikes pounding IS bases in Syria as British warplanes prepare to hit similar targets in Iraq.

At home, Chancellor George Osborne announces a two-year freeze on benefit payment levels should the Tories get back into power next May.

It was among his plans unveiled during his speech to the Conservative party conference in Birmingham.

The aim, he said, was to make £25 billion worth of further cuts to keep the economy improving. Funny how it's only him and his callous out of touch pals that think it is!

How much is that bloody new rail link going to cost again? Apparently the estimate's now risen from £32 billion to more than £40 billion for something we've managed without up to now. And what about the bill for a new war in the Middle East?

I have myself previously suggested a benefit payments freeze as a far less severe alternative to axing people's payments completely, a vicious and vindictive measure leaving many in critical financial trouble facing total ruin.

But where's the accompanying demand for prices and payments for work to also be frozen, to ensure it's not just those on welfare feeling the pinch? To single out one section of society like this is so ruddy unfair.

And I've always been very sceptical about the need for any of the government's so-called austerity measures – especially when there's no difficulty finding the cash for the HS2 rail scheme and other costly plans.

****

CHAPTER FIVE – MOCK REBELLION

You may have noticed a distinct lack of new lyrics so far in this volume of my life journal. It does seem like my muse has deserted me again, at least for the moment.

So I've decided to tweak and include a few of my old ones, putting them in the order I wrote them. I penned Beyond when I was 19 and The Magic Lingers at age 33.

Some date back to a time when I was still finding my feet and they're probably not up to the same standard as others I've already had published – particularly some that I wrote more recently. And I don't necessarily hold the same views as those expressed.

But I still think they're good enough to put out there, so to speak. So here goes…

BEYOND

Martin Money, July 10 1973 (Revised 2014)

Feeling something endless planting crystals in my mind
Slewing into cosmos, star-swept fortune cruel and kind
Fighting through the winter of a dark and gruesome war
Gaining sacred wisdom, finding miracles galore.

The serpent of the morning singing lullabies at Eve
A song of doom and darkness as the spinning spiders weave
The sparkling poison festers as the blood begins to flow
And heartbeats echo clicking of the metal god below.

Beyond – a life of garbage; beyond – the weeds of sin
Beyond – our Armageddon, into ecstasy.

An atmosphere of evil manifests into the night
As armies smash to smithereens the teachings of the light
And then the final fanfare as the Lords of Truth are seen
The races of a golden age can then wash themselves clean.

Beyond – the night of sorrow; beyond – a morning light
Beyond – the new creation; Beyond – into the One, into ecstasy.

VENUS

Martin Money, August 30, 1973 (Revised 2014)

Venus – with the sapphire eyes
Venus – brighten up my skies
Venus – how my passion cries

Venus – want you every day
Venus – come to me and stay
Oh Venus – don't you ever go away

They took away my freedom
They tried to take my mind
But I have got a passion
And it's burning up inside

Venus – with the silken hair
Venus – you're beyond compare
Oh Venus can you feel my despair?

NOT FOR SALE

Martin Money, November 27, 1976 (Revised 2014)

You can criticize my music; you can take away my cash
You can put me is a prison, you can talk a load of trash
You can make my life a nightmare; you can burn me with your hate
You can chain me to your millstone; you can leave me at the gate

But this boy won't be bought

When the vultures fly in circles, when they're ready for the kill
When the money men are knocking you can make me foot the bill
If the workers storm the palace, if the barons smash the serfs
You can let 'em fight till doomsday, they can die for all it's worth

Coz this boy won't be bought
This boy won't be bought – he's not for sale

You can love me till the daybreak, you can help me face the night
But my freedom I hold sacred – I'll be gone by morning light

Coz this boy won't be bought.

MIKE THE BIKE

Martin Money, January 2, 1977 (Revised 2014)

Mike the Bike looks like a common lout
Not the sort your ma would brag about
A face like brass, with eyes like glass
He's a hard nut, without a doubt

But when it comes to romance
He's a master of the art
Passion in his bones babe
Fire in his heart

Yeah he's a better lover than you'll ever meet
With your Rolex watch, Lotus Elite
Gin and tonic, tailored suits
Tennis club and fashion boots

Mike the Bike may seem to have no place
In your plans to save the human race
A layabout who likes to shout
Far too basic for you to face

But when it comes to romance
He's a man who knows his stuff
Gentle as a kitten, strong but never rough

Yeah he's a better lover than you'll ever meet
With your Rolex watch, Lotus Elite
Gin and tonic, tailored suits
Tennis club and fashion boots

Yeah he's a better lover than you'll ever be
With your clever words and art degree
First-class cruises, skiing trips
Sipping wine in Saint Moritz.

MEAT MARKET

Martin Money, June 3, 1977 (Revised 2014)

Glitter lights and jitter feet
Looking for a love so sweet
On the prowl for tasty meat
Down at the dance tonight

Rocking disco rolling stone
Music pounds right through your bone
It's a crime to be alone
Down at the dance tonight

It's well into the morning
The party's raving still
You wonder if you're gonna pull
You're scared you never will

Down at the dance tonight

Love making at the dance tonight
Some faking at the dance tonight
Hearts breaking at the dance tonight

Down at the dance tonight.

LOVE ON THE BEACH

Martin Money, August 4, 1977 (Revised 2014)

Pretty suntanned women lapping up the heat
Showing almost all they've got, good enough to eat

Sharp young Casanovas home in on their prey
Gonna leave their marks tonight in some virgin clay
You know what I mean

Take a trip down to the beach, there's a heaven within reach
You can suck it like a leech – on the beach

Red hot steaming passion, sun and sand and flesh
Must be something in the air, feeling kinda fresh
Lady with the lotion greasing soft brown skin
Driving all the men half-mad – see the state they're in
They're crazy for you!

Take a trip down to the beach, there's a heaven within reach
You can suck it like a leech – on the beach.

ONE DAY

Martin Money, November 6, 1977 (Revised 2014)

One day the wars will cease
One day will come the peace
One day tranquillity
One day – our destiny

The prophets of doom would have us believe
That we're lost in the ruins of Eden
Scarred fathers complain their children are nuts
And no-one's got guts to lead 'em

The peddlers of gloom are making it big
Selling shock horror probes to the masses
The dissident young have broken away
From the parents they blame for the madness

Repression depression confusion disillusion
Everyone looks so sad – it needn't be this bad

From the rubble a phoenix could rise
The storm clouds give way to sapphire skies
It's up to us, it's up to us

One day the wars will cease
One day will come the peace
One day tranquillity
One day – our destiny
One day our lives will merge
One day the single urge
One day, you, me and them
One day – Jerusalem
One day a pure unchanging light
One day to see a dazzling sight
One day we drops will form a sea
One day for all eternity
It's up to us, it's up to us.

ANGRY

Martin Money, January 1, 1978 (Revised 2014)

Angry – can't you see I'm angry
Angry – can't you see I'm angry
Tell you why

They treat us like we're animals, they call us no-good scum
They always have to put us down and stop us having fun
But baby, have you seen 'em, through that thin disguise
Suits and ties can't hide the beasts lurking in their eyes

They tell us we're degenerate and decadent and bad
They talk of moral decency and treat us like we're mad
But baby have you seen 'em – supermarket thugs
Claim to be so civilised – twice as bad as us!

Angry, can't you see I'm angry
Angry, can't you see I'm angry
And that's why

They call us lazy parasites who bleed their system dry
And ride upon their decent backs and laugh while others die
But baby just you watch 'em when the bread runs out
Savage in their selfishness while others go without

Angry, can't you see I'm angry
Angry, can't you see I'm angry
And that's why.

DON'T BE SCARED TO BE KIND

Martin Money, August 24, 1979 (Revised 2014)

*They'll hurt yer, they'll beat yer, it seems they all want to
    defeat yer*
And you ask yourself what makes 'em try destroy yer

*You've cried boy, you've bled boy, it seems they all want you
    dead boy*
Can't you see it's only rampant paranoia?

Don't be scared to be kind – it'll bring its own rewards
Don't be scared to be kind coz love cuts deeper than swords

Its cold now, it's dark now, the shadows they look so stark now
Coz a thick black wall means your love's not been woken
You've not yet discovered if warm hearts are left uncovered
It can sometimes lead to such walls being broken

Don't be scared to be kind – it'll bring its own rewards
Don't be scared to be kind coz love cuts deeper than swords

*You've cried boy, you've bled boy, it seems they all want you
    dead boy*
Can't you see it's only rampant paranoia?

Don't be scared to be kind – it'll bring its own rewards
Don't be scared to be kind coz love cuts deeper than swords

Don't be scared to be kind, it's the best thing you can do
*Don't be scared to be kind coz we've gotta, yes we've gotta push
    on through.*

MARTIAL LAW

Martin Money, February 5, 1980 (Revised 2014)

Remember the swinging sixties? – the hopes we had, the dreams
*   we shared*
The seventies saw us in retreat and now we're running scared
Iron hand in velvet glove tightened like a vice
Claws and nails them glistened through – felt as cold as ice

Before we knew what had happened gun law had seized control
The war panic mongers had us in their grasp
The bigots had won the poll

Grip of steel, dressed to kill
Serge and crease, oil and grease
No "no thanks" – join the ranks

Can't say no staring at the end of a muzzle
You're just another lump of muscle, one small piece in the puzzle
No more discos, no more rock shows
Led by psychos in the shadows
You wanna be dead heroes?

Gonna horrify our mothers, gotta fight and kill our brothers
Go to war
You're confused but there's no mystery – just a déjà vu in history
Martial law, martial law, martial law

Hail the new dark ages, back to tribal madness, martial law
Martial law (madness) martial law (madness) primal war.

BLAND MUZIK

Martin Money, July 17, 1980 (Revised 2014)

Bland muzik is all I hear
Bland muzik assaults my ear
Bland muzik all round the place
Bland muzik – a plain disgrace

Radio, TV, stereo set, air waves, thought waves clogged with it
Spineless drivel, crass nonsense, pounds and pennies,
*   bucks and cents*
Syrup-laced naivety, slogan-daubed simplicity
So pretentious, so laid back – mock rebellion, art attack

Bland muzik, so nice and neat
Bland muzik, so sickly sweet
Bland muzik set to a beat
So close your mind and move your feet

Dance away to that bland muzik
Yeah, dance away to that bland muzik
Ignore the world and dance away to that bland muzik

Can't beat 'em, so let's join 'em
Listen up – catch a load of this bland muzik
Just for you, coo-chee-coo, honey bunch, sugar babe, angel face
Ring ding, bang bang, buzz buzz, yeah yeah, oh man...

CLEAN CUT

Martin Money, October 18, 1981 (Revised 2014)

If you're gonna make a cut there's bound to be some blood
I know you don't believe me but it hurt me just as much

It was better that it ended than to carry on in pain
Coz the wine had turned to poison and our patience had been
*   drained*

I won't regret what I did; I know I'm in the right
Please think about it – what's the point in dragging out a fight?
But I'm sad, so sad, so sad

If you're gonna hate me now there's nothing I can do
I know you think I killed it but you see that's just not true

It was stone cold dead already; you can't turn back the tide
So let's just let it be now and leave the wounds inside

I won't regret what I did; I know I'm in the right
Please think about it – what's the point in dragging out a fight?
But I'm sad, so sad, so sad.

RECYCLE THE PAST

Martin Money, April 12, 1982 (Revised 2014)

(To be sung to a she-do-be-do melody)

We're into a new age; we've made it at last
Tomorrow's so doubtful, let's look to the past
Reviving the old days – Buddy and the King
When pop was so simple and love was the thing

So grease up your hair now or grow it real long
Put on your denim – sing an old song

Ooh yeah – recycle, recycle the past
Try to make it, try to make it last
Ooh yeah – recycle, recycle the past
Try to make it, try to make it last

The new waves have broken and crashed on the shore
You can try some fresh music but the oldies bring in more

So grease up your hair now or grow it real long
Put on your denim – sing an old song

Ooh yeah – recycle, recycle the past
Try to make it, try to make it last
Ooh yeah – recycle, recycle the past
Try to make it, try to make it last.

SINKING IN THE MIRE

Martin Money, May 2, 1982 (Revised 2014)

Capitulating, abdicating, I feel I'm sinking slowly in the mire

I'm slipping down, I'm sliding fast, my heart is like a stone
I'm tired and beat, can't stand this heat, the flames and pain
*   have grown*
I feel I'm sinking slowly in the mire

I've crossed the hill, I've lost the will, I'm giving up the ghost
I've had enough of fighting for the dreams I treasured most
I feel I'm sinking slowly in the mire

Capitulating, abdicating, I feel I'm sinking slowly in the mire

I'm slipping down, I'm sliding fast, my heart is like a stone
I'm tired and beat, can't stand this heat, the flames and pain
*   have grown*
I feel I'm sinking slowly in the mire

I feel I'm sinking slowly in the mire
But the slipping sand is cooler than the fire.

ACHING HEART

Martin Money, July 22, 1982 (Revised 2014)

So many friends and so many lovers
So many good time girls
No-one to talk to, sister or brother
No soul mate in the world

So many glad times, So many sad times
So many memories
So many high hopes, so many let-downs
So many shattered dreams

I need someone to ease my aching heart
Yeah I need someone to ease my aching heart

Winners and losers, surfers and boozers
Getting out of our brains
Laughing so nervous, putting an act on
Trying to soothe the pain

I need someone to ease my aching heart
Yeah I need someone to ease my aching heart.

RED SKY

Martin Money, September 30, 1983 (Revised 2014)

Red sky at night – no shepherd's delight
Wizards of darkness, snuff out the light...

...I gaze out over fields of green to chapels in the trees
The birds are singing sweetly but there's danger on the breeze

This hallowed English countryside which God was said to grace
Is due for demolition soon as fire wipes out our race

The stone is crumbling, the altars crack
The trees are wilting, the thunder's back
The sky is darkening, the sun turns red
The storm approaches to leave us dead
The birds are choking, the fields burn bright
The crosses splinter, here comes the night

I gaze out over fields of green to chapels in the trees
The birds are singing sweetly but there's danger on the breeze...

...Red sky at night – no shepherd's delight
Wizards of darkness, snuff out the light.

WE'LL BE TOGETHER

Martin Money, August 4, 1984 (Revised 2014)

One day these heavy clouds will pass, we'll sail into the dawn
We'll leave this sea of tears behind – the straits of the forlorn

Our hearts will beat as one again, from death our souls shall rise
We'll unlock doors of time between the cold Earth and the skies

Together, we'll be together, once again

One day we'll follow where you've gone, unite our family
We'll walk beside you, hold your hand throughout eternity

Together, we'll be together, once again.

DARTBOARD LOGIC

Martin Money, August 4, 1984 (Revised 2014)

Will you claim the bull's-eye? Will you score at all?
Will your aim be straight and true or will you hit the wall?
Will you net the jackpot; grab your crock of gold,
Take the star-swept glory trail and leave the mundane fold?
Or never get away?

Dartboard logic, dartboard logic – it's all so hit and miss

Buy a numbered ticket, do the pools as well
Games of luck and games of skill – snowball's chance in hell!
Brush up on your techniques, learn them golden rules
Get your home-work done on time, just like back at school
You'll never get away!

Dartboard logic, dartboard logic – it's all so hit and miss

Spin the wheel, cut the pack, gamble with your heart
Trust your soul to fickle fate on the point of a sharpened dart
It's all so hit and miss – there must be more than this!

THIS REBEL'S STILL GOT BITE

Martin Money, June 27, 1985 (Revised 2014)

*Just when you thought you'd chained me down I'm gonna rise
    again*
*Just when you thought you'd got me sussed I'll prove you wrong
    my friend*

Just when you thought you'd won my vote and clinched my loyalty
I'm gonna spoil your little game, I'm gonna break me free

Coz just as unions ain't the way
Then neither is your creed
In my mind's eye you're just as bad
You trade on human greed
The biggest axe cuts the biggest slice
But it won't get you paradise

*Just when you thought you'd bought my soul I'm gonna start to
    fight*
I ain't gonna join your ranks – this rebel's still got bite

Just as they say I've turned away and sold out to the blues
I'm gonna prove them wrong as well by coming after you

And just as the brothers disown me and Tories rub their hands
I'll pin my colours to the mast to help my fellow man
The freedom fighters have the right idea
But their savage ways are wrong I fear
As two wrongs just don't make a right
There's a far more subtle way to fight
Subversive action, change of heart,
The quiet revolution's about to start – oh yeah!

STICKS AND STONES

Martin Money, June 28, 1985 (Revised 2014)

Sticks and stones may fracture bones but do they win the fight?
The mutton-heads with steel and fire are so convinced they're right
But there's madness in their eyes as they pillage for their prize
Those crazy, crazy fools won't compromise

Blood and thunder, kill and maim is all they understand
The desp'rate rebel makes his point with the sharp blade in
*   his hand*
But with hatred in his mind the seeker will not find
The crazy, crazy tension won't unwind

Crushing the hand that feeds for a price
Axing the tree that bleeds with each slice
Chasing a dream that breeds only vice
Search your conscience – know that ain't the way.

Not a Game

Martin Money, July 14, 1986 (Revised 2014)

We can't go on tearing each other apart
Ripping the skin from our hearts
Scream as the blood-letting starts

We can't go on faking those feelings we had
Playing for laughs is so sad
Slowly it's driving us mad

I can't live with or without you
Guess you feel the same
Twisted pleasure, madcap torture
This is not a game

We can't go on hurting each other like this
Violence we cannot resist
Poison in each burning kiss

But we must go on – for us it's the only way
Made with each other to stay
Right to the very last day

I can't live with or without you
Guess you feel the same
Twisted pleasure, madcap torture
This is not a game

A shaft of sunshine, a fall of rain
A burst of passion, a stab of pain
A tender moment, a fractured shell
A glimpse of heaven, a taste of hell

This is not a game.

THE MAGIC LINGERS

Martin Money, March 3, 1987 (Revised 2014)

Time has passed, pictures faded
Linen's creased, romance jaded

Golden rings, jewel cluster
Worn and scratched, lost their lustre

The spot lit trinket show is just a memory by now
But the magic lingers on as we live a sacred vow
My love for you grows deeper every day

Champagne drunk, icing eaten
Flowers dead, weather-beaten

Veil and dress, packed for keeping
Feelings stay, never sleeping

The spot lit trinket show is just a memory by now
But the magic lingers on as we live a sacred vow
The sudden flash of fire has turned into a steady flame
Like the glow of autumn sun my emotion stays the same
Yeah my love for you grows deeper every day
This torch I'll hold for you till judgement day.

September 30 – Right, with that done, I reckon it's time for an

INTERMISSION

✳✳✳✳✳✳✳✳✳✳✳✳✳✳✳✳✳✳✳✳✳✳✳✳✳✳✳✳✳✳

DIAMONDS AND GOLD

Part Two

October to December 2014

CHAPTER SIX – GLOBAL THREATS

October 2 – There's a growing worldwide health scare over a deadly virus that has killed more than 3,000 people so far this year.

The new outbreak of Ebola started in Africa but has already spread. There's no known cure and the majority of people who contract it die.

According to the World Health Organisation, the threat to us here is minimal – but it's there all the same. The diagnosis of a guy in Texas with it this week has increased concern.

It's transmitted to humans by wild animals and then spread through direct contact with the blood, secretions, organs or other bodily fluids.

Symptoms include fever, muscle pain, headache and a sore throat followed by vomiting, diarrhoea, rash, impaired kidney and liver function and in some cases both internal and external bleeding.

Although there's no cure at present, patients can survive if they are promptly rehydrated and treated for their symptoms in hospital.

Elsewhere in the news, the search for missing Alice Gross has turned into a murder hunt following discovery of a body.

And British warplanes have now started hitting Islamic State targets in Iraq. No casualty figures have yet been released.

Oh dear – what a dangerous world we live in. But it's always been so really – even back in the 1960s hippy era.

I saw a TV programme last night on the Yesterday channel, the first of a series on that key decade – and realized to my horror how little things have changed.

There have always been flashpoints threatening world peace – Now; it's Iraq, Syria, Palestine and the Ukraine. Back then it was Vietnam, Berlin and Cuba.

Last night's programme covered the John Kennedy years – from his victory at the 1960 presidential election to his assassination in 1963.

This was the height of the Cold War between the old USSR (Russian empire) and the West, especially the United States of America. Violence, separation and the vicious enforcement of military might plagued East Germany as the wall went up in 1961.

The world came to the brink of a cataclysmic nuclear war as the USA and the Soviets squared up to each other in the Cuban Missile Crisis – only to back down just in time.

And Vietnam, a rumbling storm with the two rival super powers backing opposite sides in that country's bitter civil war, erupted in mass bloodshed and death shortly afterwards as American soldiers were thrust on to the front line.

The perceived global threats of aggressive regimes – from the Soviet Union to Islamic State – seem to be a constant feature in world history since the Second World War.

Okay, so the USSR is no more and the Berlin Wall came down in 1989. Although Russia's recent actions in Crimea have been widely condemned, East-West relations have largely thawed and are no longer seen as a likely cause of a new major conflict.

The anxiety is ever present – especially since 911 – but the identities of the major players have changed.

In the early sixties, it was Kennedy and Khrushchev, in the eighties, Reagan and Gorbachev, now its Obama and – well who exactly?

This is one of the massive problems with the volatile modern situation. Who actually is the enemy of freedom, the man or woman leading a campaign of extreme violence against the free world? Truth is we don't know because we're not being told.

Throughout history we've had identifiable enemies of democracy and freedom – Julius Caesar, Napoleon Bonaparte, Adolf Hitler, Joseph Stalin et al.

In recent times we've had a succession of bogeymen, including Idi Amin, Saddam Hussein, Osama bin Laden, Chairman Mao, Pol Pot and Radovan Karadžić.

I guess we can also add Syrian President Bashar al-Assad to that list –although the current US air strikes don't appear to be directed against either him or his supporters.

(Last year's Commons vote against air strikes in Syria followed Cameron's call for them in order to stop Assad using chemical weapons against his own people. It's said the situation's moved on since then and the current, greater threat is Islamic State.)

But now we have a vague yet violent war on terrorism with no single target person or country. We also have Islamic State – a fluid grouping of people lacking either an obvious main leader or a recognizable nation they're leading.

This, I feel, is a doubly dangerous state of affairs. At least with Hitler and Germany we had a proper perception of whom and what we were fighting. Not that war is ever desirable of course.

As the TV programme about the sixties illustrated so well, we've always had battles, brutal regimes, bloodshed and civil unrest somewhere or other on this crazy globe.

But modern crises are less well defined. The battle lines are flexible and the conflicts seemingly unending   and that's very, very scary.

And that suits the evil manipulators wielding the most power just fine. They stay firmly in charge while coaxing us to fight each other instead of challenging them.

Even the short-lived peace and love era – no doubt featured in later shows in the telly series – ended abruptly with violent student riots, Vietnam and the grisly murder of a Rolling Stones fan by Hell's Angels at a concert by the rock group at Altamont, USA.

October 3 – I watched the whole of Prime Minister David Cameron's speech to the Conservative Party conference the other day.

He came across as supremely confident and used language that sounded very reasonable – even cracking a few jokes at Ed Miliband's expense.

He spoke passionately about wanting to protect the National Health Service and appeared quite angry that Labour MPs were claiming he did not care about it.

It was powerful and persuasive, reeking of common sense and compassion.

Even I started to wonder if maybe he wasn't as bad as harsh critics like me had always believed he was.

But then I thought hold on, he's preaching to the converted here – a hall full of people who clearly idolize him, fully support his policies and gave him a standing ovation before he'd even started speaking (and another when he finished).

It would have been a very different story had he been facing the general public badly hit by and totally fed up with his awful administration and the devastation it's caused.

And what is it with this zealous hero worship anyway? Party conferences used to be a chance for delegates to debate matters – with sometimes fiercely clashing opinions – then pass resolutions. There was real cut and thrust as vital issues were thrashed out.

Now they seem far too slick, stage managed and mock showbiz with not a trace of disagreement, dissent or heckling. And that applies to all of them, not just the Tories. It's an affront to democracy.

But any doubts that might have crept in to my mind that maybe I'd been giving smooth-talking David an unjustly hard time were completely crushed this morning when I saw two items on the BBC TV news that made me seethe.

One was about Tory plans to stop British laws being overruled by human rights rulings from Strasbourg.

While I'd be the first to applaud any moves challenging the European super state's high-handed meddling, trying to tell us how to run our own country, I'm deeply concerned that it's Cameron's Conservatives involved here.

As always with that shower, it's the motive behind the motion that makes me shudder. I strongly suspect yet another attempt to erode our civil liberties and control us more.

The second news item centred on another Tory proposal that on the face of it sounded good but similarly threatened to betray the party's true colours.

It said the government had launched four pilot schemes to help unemployed people with mental health problems back into the workplace.

Apparently, they will see some people on Employment and Support Allowance being offered tailor-made career advice and psychiatric help.

The £2 million pilots, all in England, will run for six months. It's claimed they'll be voluntary, not compulsory – and if only that were true, I for one would be in favour.

But I'm very anxious about just how much pressure will be put on the cerebrally fragile to comply or lose their benefits.

And one Conservative MP interviewed said it would help those with mental health issues fulfil their potential and become fully-functioning members of society again rather than being a burden on the welfare state.

What a knob! He might have got away with it had he stopped talking at the end of the first, very positive section of his statement, which I and others would wholeheartedly support – but he simply couldn't resist adding the very revealing second part.

So once again, we get to the real issue for true blue Tories. Cameron can bang on about supporting the NHS and the welfare state till the cows come home, but when you strip away the rhetoric and get down to brass tacks, both cost a lot of money and the Conservatives want to reduce their funding no matter who suffers in the process.

In fact, thinking about it, he did as good as admit this in his conference speech when he said the economy had to be strong in order to support a strong, efficient NHS.

Rubbish! Services looking after our health and welfare should be run according to citizens' requirements – never, ever using cold profit and loss criteria like commercial companies operating in the harsh business world. That's immoral.

But for Tories it's all about sod the people; let's balance the books – unless wars abroad or shiny new rail schemes are involved of course.

Welcome to England, PLC your local branch of Britain Enterprises, itself a subsidiary of Europe International. Ye gods!

October 4 – We woke up this morning to the shocking news that an English aid worker had been beheaded in Syria.

The BBC told us that a video showing the gruesome atrocity had been put out by Islamic State members who claimed that Alan Henning, from Eccles near Manchester, was killed because he was a spy working undercover.

This is hotly denied by his family and friends who said the former taxi driver was a kind man who had felt driven to go out and help the beleaguered people of that war-torn country.

He was working alongside Muslims to ease suffering, they said. And indeed Islamic community leaders in England have been quick to condemn his barbaric slaughter.

I'd suggest that it's highly unlikely that Mr Henning was a spy. But it is possible, and once again we're being asked to trust that what we're being told is the truth.

And the cynic in me can't help noticing that this stunning act of savagery has played right into the hands of the politicians who have been indecently quick off the mark to further demonize IS and justify their own warlike activities in the Middle East.

But any way you look at it, the deliberate butchering of this man was an act of pure evil. It goes way beyond politics and religion and is firmly in the realm of the crazed and psychotic.

It's so sickening it's almost unbelievable. Our thoughts are with his nearest and dearest at this tragic time.

But let's remember that Islamists don't have a monopoly over crazed and psychotic words and deeds. Murderous nuts can be found in all extreme religious or political groupings. And, dare I say, even in the corridors of Whitehall and the White House.

Peace-loving people of all persuasions need to stand up and say enough is enough. Tolerance and mutual respect are desperately needed if we're ever going to move forward towards a world finally living in harmony.

Will that ever happen? – Quite probably not, but surely we must strive for that ideal. Otherwise we just carry on hating and fighting, maiming and murdering – whether such activities are sanctioned by any recognized state or not. Either way we all lose.

October 5 – Happy golden birthdays Joe and Cheryl – my ex-wife and her twin sister born exactly 50 years ago today. And happy silver birthday greetings go out to Emily, my daughter-in-law, who's 25.

I find it intriguing that my son and I both married women born on this date – and therefore his wife's birthday is the same day as his mum's. Phil's own silver celebration is next month – November 22.

So we have silver birthdays to add to the ruby, golden and diamond ones being marked by me, my family and friends this year – with more to come next year.

Glittering times for brilliant people.

On a more serious note, we learned today that a man's body had been found in London – believed to be the guy who killed Alice Gross.

October 10 – Earlier today I got back from a few days away in a caravan in Weymouth with friends.

I had a very pleasant, chilled and relaxing break at Haven's Sea View site – the same one we went to in September last year. (See *Volume Seven, Persistent Illusions*.)

But unfortunately it was not so good for others.

Once again I went there with Sam, Carl and family – but this time minus her cousin Jac, being accompanied instead by Tina Mcauley, Jem Hannen and Becca's friend Joedie along with Bec's terrier dog Albert and Joedie's baby girl Lillie.

Poor Sam wasn't at all well so she, Carl, Rudy and Bailey returned to Bournemouth on Wednesday.

Alex and his girlfriend Charley were also present Monday and Tuesday but they too went home Wednesday.

The rest of us stayed on until this morning. Like I said, for me personally it was a lovely five days away and a nice break from normal routine. But it's so, so good to be back home!

October 11 – Ey up, a brand new lyric's popped into my head. Here goes:

THE TOXIC SIDE OF ME

Martin Money, October 11, 2014

I dunno what it is coz I'm a kind man as a rule
But when I'm in your presence jokes and comments get quite cruel
My language is abrasive and my attitude stone hard
Yeah people see the toxic side of me

I love when we're together and the way you make me smile
You're crazy and amusing and I really like your style
While hanging out with others I'm a lot more sweet and nice
But when we get together chilled demeanour turns to ice
And people see the toxic side of me

The toxic side of me
The toxic side of me
Yeah people see the toxic side of me

I try to keep it hidden but you find it every time
You pick it till it bleeds and what seeps out's corrosive slime
As people see the toxic side of me

I wish I could control it and I know how hard I've tried
I feel so schizophrenic like a Jekyll with a Hyde
I cannot really blame you as it's my fault I'm like this
And people see the toxic side of me.

I've been thinking more about the shocking media story concerning the beheading of English aid worker Alan Henning – and especially a comment made by a bloke on TV last night.

This feller was basically berating Islamic State, saying we couldn't tolerate such barbaric behaviour in a civilised world so we basically had no choice now but to send in our troops to stop it committing such atrocities.

Apart from thinking how well our own government's propaganda had worked on this guy – and no doubt many other unquestioning souls accepting the official version of events without hesitation – I immediately saw several massive flaws in his reasoning.

Firstly, I wondered why the heck he thought it was our job to act as agents of humanity and justice on another nation's soil.

We wouldn't take too kindly to such a brash intervention in our own affairs by outsiders enraged by our way of doing things here, would we? No, we'd lock them up and throw away the key.

Ah yes, some would be quick to point out, but Mr Henning was no violent troublemaking intruder but a kind, innocent man trying to help Syrian people.

This is by far the most likely scenario but I've already stated that we never know for sure whether we're being told the whole truth. I'd wager he was neither a spy nor an undercover subversive but such folk could and probably would pose as aid workers.

And you could argue that those going to a volatile war zone to help citizens are risking their lives just as much as the military. It's appalling I know but sadly true.

Such a brutal execution of anyone for any reason at all is just plain evil and incredibly barbaric – whether or not it's sanctioned by a community.

Which brings me to point two – the growing clamour of calls in our own land for those committing certain crimes to be hanged or brutalized.

Well, apart from pointing out that at present we're not allowed to re-introduce the death penalty under European law, I ask you, how frigging hypocritical is that?

Especially if those slating IS extermination methods are the same folk demanding the return of capital punishment here – which in my experience is quite likely!

And if you're going to kill someone, it makes little difference to them whether you decapitate them, shoot them, blow them up, poison or electrocute them – they're still dead. Some types of execution are seen as more humane and less savage, that's all.

Point three concerns the whole issue of dying. Some depart this level of existence on a battlefield, others in terrorist attacks, and many in fatal accidents. Most do it peacefully in beds either at home or hospital after falling prey to natural causes.

It's largely the luck of the draw and when your time's up, it's up.

A lethal injection, voltage charge or dose of poison ends a life a lot quicker – and therefore considerably more mercifully – than having someone bear the pain, humiliation, frustration and misery of a drawn-out demise through terminal illness.

Much the same could apply to switching off a life support machine in certain circumstances.

As my dear old Dad said on facing his own mortality, it's the quality of life that matters, not its quantity.

I would also argue that chopping off someone's head is also a much faster and far less cruel way of ending their days than crucifying, torturing or starving them – providing it's done from behind and unexpectedly, not from the front after lengthy tormenting.

Having said that, I totally agree that being beheaded is a particularly brutal, gruesome and shocking way to go. It's so damned horrific and primitive – a totally unwanted relic from a dark and bloody past that has no place in the modern world.

But aristocrats were famously and notoriously separated from their bony skulls on a regular basis during the French Revolution as late as the 18th century.

And Islamic State isn't the only culprit these days. Various communities still decapitate perceived wrongdoers including our old friends, firm allies and huge benefactors the Saudis – yet we don't hear calls to bomb or invade them, do we?

Nor should we, I hasten to add!

And let's face it, criminals still die in state-sanctioned electric chairs in America, and the rope was the ultimate penalty in this country until that law was finally abolished in 1998, although the last actual justice-system hanging took place in 1964.

At the end of the day, execution is execution. You're committing the ultimate act of killing someone. It's ultra-violent, evil extermination – whichever way you look at it, try to dress it up or whatever method's used.

October 13 – Hospital staff staged a four-hour walk-out today in protest over the government's disgraceful refusal to increase their pay by a measly one per cent.

Yes, one per cent – as MPs propose to award themselves a 10 per cent rise. Talk about bare faced cheek! Actually it's worse than that – far worse. It's abhorrent!

Ambulance services faced disruption and non-urgent minor operations were delayed as a result of the first pay strike by NHS staff in England for 32 years.

Many health workers were apparently torn over the decision to take such drastic action inconveniencing patients. But they felt it was the only way to get the politicians to listen. This is awful.

Nurses shouldn't have to feel so emotionally blackmailed and compromised. Like police officers, fire fighters, soldiers and other vital front-line servants of society, they should be placed in a special category with its own rules.

They should be so well respected and treated that they never feel such grievances or the need to take industrial action to have them addressed.

These people don't do their jobs for the money. They're not greedy. They just want justice – to feel that governments recognize their great worth to us all and reflect it in fair pay structures and working conditions.

Anyone who's read Scalpels and Angels will know I have my own deeply personal reasons to be full of admiration, respect and eternal gratitude for hard-pressed nurses and hospital workers who do such sterling work in sometimes difficult conditions.

Bleeding hell, I'm getting quite misty-eyed writing this. It's an emotional subject.

So you can imagine my rage at the hard-hearted attitude of the politicians – and their ridiculous assertions in blocking the one per cent pay rise.

Health secretary Jeremy Hunt had the amazing temerity to warn today that up to 15,000 nurses would need to be laid off if the government permitted the increase.

What total bollocks!

This isn't the health workers' intention at all and I can't believe he's got the gall to imply that it is. Apart from their request for a very modest pay rise, they are also pretty fed up with working long shifts because they're always UNDER-STAFFED!

Out of touch idiot!

Oh, and so much for Cameron's passionate speech at the Conservative Party conference praising and defending the NHS. That didn't last long, did it? Put your money where your mouth is, mate!

Or rather, our money we trust you to spend where it's most needed.

Ah, but times are hard and the cash isn't there to fund a pay rise, they say. Well, it is, but it's needed for a new war and a high speed rail track. You don't mind, do you?

Well, actually, they don't give a monkey's if we do. They're okay, so are their wealthy mates who look after them as long as they're lots of pandering going on. Sod the rest of us, especially if we're ill, serving the community, low-paid, poverty-stricken or on benefits.

The starting salary for a registered nurse is £21,478 a year. Yet a 10 per cent pay rise for MPs is likely to go ahead next year after the head of Parliament's expenses watchdog claimed their "miserly" £67,000 wage was not enough! You frigging what?

In addition to these generous salaries, many MPs have considerable personal wealth and can always use their positions to secure cash and favours from all over the place.

Unbelievable! Or at least it would be if we hadn't already been staggered many times by the words and actions of these coalition creeps. They're behaving like despicable, cold-blooded reptiles; it's as simple as that.

Just when we think they've reached a new low and can't possibly sink any lower, they manage to do just that with unsettling and upsetting ease.

What a nasty, spiteful bunch of gits they are – issuing veiled threats that giving in to the nurses' more than reasonable pay rise call would force them to sack thousands of health workers when the service needs more care staff, not fewer. That's evil.

Such a vindictive move would throw even more unfortunate folk on to the mercy of the benefits system just as these dreadful politicians are outrageously claiming unemployment's falling (yeah, course it is!).

And if it truly was, and if the economy was actually recovering as they keep telling us, then surely they could accommodate the modest NHS pay increase? And they wouldn't be announcing even more cuts should they get back into power next May.

Do they really think we're that stupid, to swallow all their lies and bullshit? It's highly insulting that they treat us all with such contempt.

They do occasionally – very occasionally – come up with a good idea that improves life for citizens. But it's usually because it will somehow benefit them, not us.

Oh, by the way, before we leave the nurses pay topic I feel the need to clarify something.

I've constantly made known my deep scepticism at the alleged need for an austerity drive, feeling it's simply another stick to beat us with.

My suspicions appear to have been confirmed by the sudden miraculous appearance of billions of pounds for HS2 and the apparent total absence of any government reservations about the high cost of fighting another war in the Middle East.

But, in chapter four, responding to George Osborne's planned two-year freeze on benefits levels, I did point out that I had actually earlier suggested this as a far less drastic, much fairer alternative to axing some people's welfare payments altogether.

I added that if savings were necessary, which I've always doubted, such a benefits standstill should be accompanied by a similar freezing of work payment levels and goods and services pricing, so benefit claimants didn't feel discriminated against.

Just to make sure I'm not misunderstood, I was referring to the pay levels of commercial, retail, business and other general categories not nurses, fire fighters, soldiers, police officers and other invaluable servants of society I'd put in my suggested special sector.

Because people like that are a special breed. They're invaluable. And the sooner governments realize this and recognize it in practical terms, the better.

****

CHAPTER SEVEN – THE POSSESSED

October 14 – Hate is such a powerful word, don't you think?

It probably looks like I feel that strong emotion towards the coalition politicians, considering how vivid and unflattering my language can become when commenting on their ghastly words and behaviour.

I might have even said that I hate Cameron, Osborne, Clegg and company more than once when my anger and disgust have run away with me.

But I don't really hate them – as people. I can't because I don't know them. I just see how they come across in public – what they say and do.

They all no doubt have their good qualities and may well be nice guys in their private lives. I said at the time I really felt for David Cameron as a person when his poorly six-year-old son Ivan died on my 55th birthday in 2009 (See the Cynical Optimist).

At the deepest level we're all human beings and we can empathize with each other's tragedies and traumas – unless we're completely mad, heartless or weird, that is.

But most of the time we just react to each other's surface personas as displayed in words and actions. And it's at this level I have real problems with Cameron and crew.

It's as if they frequently become possessed by malevolent and highly destructive force while meeting in Parliament and Whitehall. They're controlled and guided by it and speak and act accordingly.

Where this force emanates from is open to debate. But I'm convinced it lurks in the dark shadows of the corridors of power, where self-obsessed, sick and twisted individuals manipulate the elected politicians like malleable puppets.

For myself, I've said many times that I don't like it at all when anyone's words or actions upset me to the point I get all steamed up and un-spiritual. I abhor such negative vibes and much prefer to try and spread the love we all so desperately need.

Phew! – Heavy stuff, eh?

On a much lighter note, I'd like to wish a very happy birthday to Christine Jones and Steve Gray, two long-time friends dating back to the golden years of the Home Guard Social Club and Pinecliff, Palmerston, Portman and White Horse pubs in the 1980s.

Turning to today's news, the sister of British hostage John Cantlie has pleaded with his Islamic State captors to resume contact with her family after recently severing it.

Mr Cantlie, 43, was captured in northern Syria in late 2012 while working as an independent photojournalist.

His sister, Jessica said she was making the appeal on behalf of her father, Paul, who is "terminally ill and incapacitated" and made his own plea from his sick bed earlier this month.

The sibling told the kidnappers: "We had previously been in contact through a channel started by you, but then this stopped for reasons best known to you.

"Sadly, like the families of David Haines and Alan Henning before they were killed, our efforts at re-opening dialogue continue to be ignored by those holding John.

"We strongly challenge those holding John to return to your previously opened channel, to which we continue to send messages and await your response so that in keeping with everyone's wishes, we can restart dialogue."

John Cantlie, dressed in an orange jumpsuit, appeared in a propaganda video released by IS on Sunday in which he addressed the issue of air strikes by the West in Iraq.

He said: "Anyone hoping for a nice neat surgical operation without getting their hands dirty is in for a horrible surprise once it gets under way."

Our nation has been shocked and appalled in recent weeks on hearing that aid workers David Haines and Alan Henning had both been beheaded.

We all sympathise deeply with Mr Cantlie's family and fear he will meet the same grisly end. But Jessica's use of the very pointed words "strongly challenge" is both interesting and very alarming.

And her appearance in the video requesting Islamic State to re-establish contact in the hope a deal can be struck to save her brother's life was strange to say the least.

This was not the image of a tearful, deeply distressed sibling pleading for clemency, as you might expect. She seemed far too composed – there was a distinct lack of raw emotion and she looked poker-faced.

Linked with the term "strongly challenge", it left the distinct impression she was confronting Mr Cantlie's captors, goading and defying them, throwing down the gauntlet if you like.

Okay, she did add "we implore IS to reinitiate direct contact." But the whole tone of the filmed appeal lacked the feel of a peaceful, humble, conciliatory plea for mercy.

I don't blame her for this at all. The poor woman must be beside herself worrying about her brother and her dad. But she had clearly been told not to show it.

Her video request was no doubt heavily doctored and largely phrased by the security services and she had quite obviously been instructed not to display any emotion, desperation or sign of weakness that might play right into the hands of John's captors.

If Mr Cantlie is still alive, his fate is pretty much sealed now. Had there been a flicker of hope he would be released to return home safely, it was snuffed out by that ill-informed video. I fear it's actually signed his death warrant. And that's so sad and horrific.

October 15 – I saw that terrible work-placed pension advert again on telly yesterday evening. You know the one – it shows groups of workers in various settings shouting "we're in" like brainless parrots while acting like comatose sheep.

It really makes me cringe, as it illustrates so very well the sort of society politicians want to be leading. One in which everyone thinks, acts and speaks exactly the same, no-one breaks ranks or shows even a trace of individuality or imagination.

People are little more than numbers – meek, compliant unthinking slaves to a cruel, unrelenting system run for the benefit of the privileged all-powerful few in charge.

While obedient to authority, these blinkered and brainwashed sheep are fiercely competitive among themselves, relentlessly vying for position – eternal wannabes who'll never make it because the system's rigged against them.

This is Utopia for the government, but it resembles a Hell on Earth to me.

Once again I envisage the immediate response – it's only a TV ad for goodness' sake, lighten up Money!

But I find it sinister in the extreme that vivid images like this are incorporated in TV commercials – this one put out by a government department. Talk about Big Brother!

Such insidious but powerful ideas are planted in the subconscious until we start thinking this is perfectly normal, the way things should be.

Other adverts and media projects carry equally strong and sinister subliminal messages so we end up wondering if there's something wrong with us if we don't share these warped mindsets. At that point, the puppet-masters have us in their thrall.

All this scares the crap out of me, I can tell you!

Something else I watched on TV last night was another programme in the Yesterday channel's series about the 1960s.

This one centred on the Vietnam War debacle with all its violence, cock-ups, blood, pain, protest, tragedy and misery.

The film footage of poor native innocents caught up in the highly-destructive insanity brought back my own memories of the so-called Vietnamese Boat People.

This was the name given to refugees who fled that country by sea in the wake of the war, especially during 1978 and 1979, but continuing into the 1990s.

My own poignant personal experience with some of them came in 1979 when I was working as a reporter for the *Christchurch Times* weekly newspaper.

I was despatched with a photographer to an old RAF camp at Sopley in the New Forest – just within the paper's circulation area – to meet the first group of refugees arriving there to be temporarily housed while homes were found for them elsewhere.

It was a major story attracting nationwide media attention. But the authorities simply weren't permitting a close-up mass intrusion into the wrecked lives of these poor traumatised Vietnamese people spending their first hours in a strange new country.

Consequently, all the TV camera crews, Fleet Street hacks, photographers and freelancers had been ushered out of the base by lunchtime.

But, as local journalists whose papers enjoyed a good relationship with RAF Sopley's bosses, a Bournemouth Echo reporter called Mike Goodey and me were secretly invited to stay on in the afternoon to meet some of the refugees settling in to their new homes in huts at the base.

The Sopley chiefs knew we would be a lot more sensitive than hard-bitten national media guys and the Vietnamese could probably handle a couple of discreet local journalists but not the blaze of publicity, crush and mayhem of earlier in the day.

So off we went with an interpreter to be introduced to some of the families. To say it was an incredibly moving and humbling experience would be a huge understatement.

These poor people had come 7,000 miles across the globe in the most atrocious of conditions to settle in an alien land. Life would never be the same again. They must have been deeply anxious, wondering what the heck lay ahead.

And yet, when we arrived at their door, what was one of the first things they did? Offer us a cup of tea.

Blimey! I was knocked sideways. These people were lucky to be alive and coming to terms with fleeing for their lives from their homeland to take a nightmare journey to a new country on the other side of the world.

Yet their first instinct was to share this most communal, unifying, ordinary custom.

This was amazing proof of the strength and resilience of the human spirit. It made me feel ashamed at moaning and bitching about stuff that seemed important but immediately paled into insignificance on meeting these incredible people.

My short time with those friendly, hospitable families was one of the most life-affirming and enlightening experiences I ever had in my quarter-century as a journalist. All I can say in summary is – Wow!

Coming bang up to date, we've had yet another glaring example in today's news of hard-hearted Tory thinking – the spiteful mentality lurking behind this coalition government.

Welfare minister Lord Freud has been forced to apologize for something he said at the recent Conservative Party conference in Birmingham in which he suggested that some disabled people should not be entitled to the minimum wage.

Labour has demanded his resignation and Cameron was quick to distance himself from the peer's remarks, saying they "were not the views of anyone in government".

But this guy's one of your ministers Dave – in the welfare department at that!

Lord Freud today apologized unreservedly, saying he was "foolish" to make such comments, which he admitted could be seen as offensive. But he refused to quit.

Cameron can protest all he likes, but I feel this is yet another case of a Tory in government letting slip the real hard line agenda behind the reasoned rhetoric.

In other words, showing the Conservatives' true blue colours – the colours of the selfish, privileged, callous elite running our country for their own benefit while screwing the rest of us at every opportunity.

October 16 – There's a long-held and persistent belief in mainstream UK culture that Conservative is the party of the individual while Labour is the champion of the co-operative community.

It might have seemed that way once, but that's far too simplistic for my liking.

Such crude stereotypes suit some shrewd manipulators right down to the ground. Me? – I'd say the reality's a lot more subtle and multi-faceted than that.

Take my comments yesterday about that ghastly work-placed pensions ad for example. Some might well have gone away with the impression I was being a bit Tory and decidedly anti-socialist in complaining about the dull uniformity and acquiescence being displayed and bemoaning the lack of free-thinking originality.

Not so. I see no conflict between my firm belief in strong, creative individualism and my vision of a world where citizens live in unity, peace and harmony showing respect and tolerance for others.

You can be bold and imaginative, independent-minded and even visionary while still playing your part in a mutually-supportive society based firmly on fairness, justice, diversity of skills and equality of opportunities.

Those who think the two are incompatible are playing right into the hands of the divide and rule merchants who mercifully exploit people's different worldviews and lifestyles to cause arguments, friction and confrontations.

And, let's face it; Labour governments in recent times have been more like Tory administrations than anything reflecting the red brigade's traditional socialist roots.

Meanwhile, the blue rosette crowd have shown that they are just as keen to rule over a community where everyone thinks and acts exactly the same, doing as they're told and quietly toeing the line while dreaming in vain of freeing themselves from the shackles that bind them and keep them oppressed.

In other words, aspiring to higher things as they perceive them but never succeeding – except for the chosen few hand-picked to join that exclusive club.

Me, I'd like to see communities run using the finest qualities of conservative, socialist and liberal thinking overridden by a distinctly Green outlook caring for citizens, animals and the environment while investing power in the people at grass-roots levels.

A place where individuals can truly be themselves but not at the expense of others.

This is the total antithesis of our current set-up where the super-rich, the greedy bankers and massive, powerful multinationals run the show.

Where politicians lie and cheat to gain and attain positions in government and the business, education, administrative, media and entertainment sectors are all dominated by hard cash, superficiality, uniformity, box-ticking and rigid unimaginative formulas.

It's the shallow domain of slick, stage-managed party conferences, sound bites, CCTV, a biased, scandal-obsessed Fleet Street, social networking psychos and pseudos, bland, safe pop music, cruel, brash, tedious telly talent shows and mind-numbing reality series making unthinking self-centred fools overnight celebrities.

Sadly, a place where that dreadful pensions advert and other highly suspect media initiatives fit in perfectly.

October 20 – The nation's favourite "Oxo mum" Lynda Bellingham has died aged 66 after battling cancer.

The actress and TV presenter was best known for playing a gravy-loving family's matriarch in the long-running advert for the popular stock cubes.

She also appeared in various programmes including All Creatures Great and Small, and was in later years a regular on the daytime chat show Loose Women.

Tributes have poured in for a lady said to have been a true professional and a lovely person.

Returning to my disgust at the government's refusal to grant health workers a paltry one per cent increase, I pointed out the other day that the starting salary for a registered nurse is apparently a modest £21,478 a year against an MP's £67,000 – before all their added perks, of course.

Yet while blocking the one per cent bid by invaluable hard-pressed front line hospital staff, the avaricious and selfish parliamentarians look like giving themselves a 10 per cent pay rise next year. That's disgraceful!

But something on today's news made me remember that there are many more people getting astronomical payments dwarfing the MPs' salaries – just for entertaining us.

Top professional footballers, for example, can command over £200,000 A WEEK and the average for a Premier League player is £31,000 a week. And it's hardly what you'd call full-time work.

Like millions, I love the beautiful game and watching its most skilled performers. But come on, that's frigging ridiculous!

I've said it before and I'll say it again – set a minimum wage by law to help protect workers' rights, but please set a maximum salary as well in each sector of society. No-one should be that well off when others are poverty-stricken or on the streets. That's just plain immoral!

Some bonehead will no doubt chime in here that setting such a glass ceiling would discourage the best people from striving for excellence. Rubbish! – Not all brilliantly skilled, wonderfully creative and visionary people are that greedy, and to suggest they are is a gross insult.

Let me ask a question. Do you think it's right that sports and pop stars are paid such colossal sums while life-saving nurses struggle financially in a critically understaffed profession and savagely discarded people who put their lives on the line in battle zones are homeless, sleeping under cardboard in shop doorways?

Because I bloody well don't!

I take my hat off to those who run and man soup kitchens and provide food and bedding, giving up their own time to assist unfortunate casualties of an uncaring system. Or indeed anyone who volunteers to help others – in hospitals or wherever.

October 21 – World-famous South African athlete Oscar Pistorius was this morning sentenced to five years in prison for the death of

Reeva Steenkamp as his televised seven month trial finally came to an end.

He was given a concurrent suspended three-year jail sentence for a firearms offence.

The judge at Pretoria's High Court ruled that he would have to serve a minimum of one-sixth of the five years – meaning he could be released under supervision (house arrest) after 10 months if a parole request is subsequently made and granted.

He could also be let out on bail pending an appeal if his defence team lodges one – although such an inquiry could take several months to be arranged and heard anyway.

Paralympic champion sprinter Pistorius, 27, who has no lower legs and runs using devices called blades, admitted shooting Reeva, his girlfriend, at his Pretoria home on Valentine's Day, 14 February, 2013.

But he told the court it was a tragic accident and he fired at what he thought was intruders. It was one of the most high-profile trials in history.

He was convicted of culpable homicide – what we call manslaughter – after being cleared of murder.

While some – including Reeva's family and friends – will no doubt be incensed at the perceived leniency of the sentence, the judge said she had taken into account Pistorius' version of the incident, his formerly unblemished record, his inspirational influence on young disabled athletes and his charity work.

As I've already said, I, too, firmly believe in balancing a person's wrongdoings against any good deeds they've performed helping others. This reflects the natural law of karma that works on this golden principle.

October 23 – Happy birthday to my nephew Richard Dixon and to my friend Sharon Pendleton. But as a sharp contrast, we've learned of yet another celebrity death, this time of glam rocker Alvin Stardust.

Born Bernard Jewry in Muswell Hill, London, he was a singer and actor for decades but is best known for his leather-clad rocker persona during the seventies glam era. Recently diagnosed with cancer, he died after a short illness. He was 72.

Alvin's two biggest hits were My Coo-Ca-Choo (number two) and Jealous Mind (number one) as he reached the top ten seven times in the 1970s and 1980s. He also appeared in a road safety advert and in various acting roles on telly.

He'd not long finished a new album, due out next month.

October 25 – Yesterday was pretty flipping stupendous! Why? – Because I saw my bro and sis Tom and Christine Jones for the first time in ages. They came over for the day from their Southampton home and stayed last night in a Bournemouth hotel.

They arrived at my place just before lunchtime and we had a coffee and catch-up before going to Quarters burger restaurant in Southbourne for a meal.

After that, they booked in to their three-star accommodation and went shopping for the afternoon before we hooked up again for a very pleasant evening in the Litten Tree disco pub in Bournemouth town centre.

Chris kindly collected me in her car and then parked it at the hotel, a short walk from the pub, so she could have a few drinks. Our mutual buddy Steve Gray – someone else I hadn't seen in yonks – met us there with a mate of his.

It was fantastic being reunited with close friends I've known for donkey's years, proudly swapping information about our families, having a laugh and reminiscing over a pint or three – without a doubt one of the highlights of my year so far.

October 26 – I've lit a candle and I'm playing a Cream CD in honour of Jack Bruce, the legendary bass guitarist and singer who shot to fame with "rock's first super group" in the late 1960s. He died yesterday aged 71 from liver disease.

Born in May 1943 at Bishopbriggs, Scotland, Bruce was a much in-demand musician, playing with a long list of famous names during his half-century career, including Manfred Mann, Graham Bond, Alexis Korner, John Mayall, Robin Trower, Rory Gallagher, Charlie Watts, Gary Moore, Lou Reed, Frank Zappa and Ringo Starr.

But he's best known for his work with lead guitarist Eric Clapton and drummer Ginger Baker in Cream, a groundbreaking rock-blues-jazz outfit that sold 35 million albums in just over two years from 1966 to 1969, including the first ever platinum disc – the double platter Wheels of Fire, comprising a live recording and a studio set.

Bruce and Cream were highly influential – David Bowie, Ella Fitzgerald and Jimi Hendrix covered his songs and tributes have come in across the board, from Geezer Butler of Black Sabbath to Yusuf Islam (Cat Stevens) to ex- Sex Pistol Steve Jones.

Some of Cream's most famous tracks were written by Bruce and Peter Brown, including White Room, Politician, I Feel Free and Sunshine of Your Love (in which Clapton also had a hand).

RIP Jack – and thanks for the music.

Turning briefly to other news, British troops officially finished their combat role in Afghanistan today and handed over Camp Bastion to the local security forces.

Good – they should never have been sent there in the first place.

It brings to an end a costly 13-year campaign in which 453 of our service personnel lost their lives and many more were maimed and mentally scarred.

No official figure has been released for the total number of Afghan civilian casualties, but it's thought to be up to 20,000.

How tragic. Now the big debate starts – was it worth it? And can we sleep more safely in our beds as a result?

I'd say absolutely not on both counts. If anything, we're in a more perilous state than ever, given our political leaders' obsession with meddling in foreign affairs, enraging other nations and cultures and consequently making us even more of a target.

And at the end of all that bloodshed and misery, we're told that the Taliban – the perceived enemy said to have harboured Al Qaeda terrorists after 911 – haven't been defeated, just contained. So in other words it could all flare up again.

In which case, we'd have a moral responsibility now to intervene again and help sort out the mess, because we'd be more than partly responsible for it after sending in our troops. Just like in the Iraq crisis.

The official line is that our job is done – Afghanistan is now a stable democracy able to deal with its own internal problems. But up to 1,000 service folk will remain there to continue training and supporting the native military and security forces.

The cynic in me would argue that the real reason is that, with coalition cutbacks stretching our service personnel and resources to the limit, those people and that equipment will soon be deployed in combat mode in Iraq and Syria.

So the bitter and bloody ideological war will drag on – only the backdrop will change. And this will increasingly put us all in grave danger with the very real threat of backlash terrorist attacks on our own soil. Great!

Cheers Dave, George and Nick. You're doing a grand job in protecting your country from harm!

October 28 – I was watching an old episode of New Tricks on TV's Alibi channel last night in which one of the characters called another "Tich."

My thoughts immediately turned to my dear old Dad; for this was his siblings' nickname for him (I've inherited his lack of height).

My cousin Sandra also irreverently called him "Tich" – mind you, she also insisted in calling our Auntie Joyce "Joycie", our uncle Fred "Freddie" and her own father, my uncle Bert, "Georgie." He hated his middle name of George and she couldn't resist winding him up.

But then we were that sort of family I guess – always ribbing each other playfully with all love. And laughing a lot.

October 29 – I'm currently reading a book called *SOS – Alternatives to Capitalism*, written by Canadian journalist and activist Richard Swift, whose specialist subjects include ecology and democracy. It's both absorbing and thought-provoking

It starts by stating the obvious – our current global economic set-up based on hard cash and materialism is unfair, unsatisfactory and un-sustainable. An urgent, radical change is needed for all our sakes – including other species and the planet itself.

And it explodes many myths – including the one that the only alternative to our prevailing sharp-edged, soulless, joyless, divisive form of capitalism is the harsh, soulless, joyless iron-fist communism as used by the old Soviet Union and Red China.

Swift also challenges the popular assumption that people living in so-called primitive societies before the industrial revolution were less happy than us. He further asserts that some communities were a lot more caring and democratic and people generally had more leisure time.

A lot of what he says accords with my own view that we desperately require a new set-up replacing cash obsession, reckless resource plundering and blatantly unfair wealth distribution with a more truly democratic system infused with compassion, humour, mutual support and care for other creatures and our nurturing Mother Earth.

I guess this is one of the main reasons I'm unnerved by the statements of the Illuminati guy on his comprehensive website promoting the New World Order. His vision of a future replacing democracy with meritocracy seems far too cold, clinical, soulless and intolerant to me. Quite brutal, in fact.

Oh, and just to clarify – I ain't no Luddite, calling for a return to feudal living conditions before electricity or running water. I have no problem with modern science or cutting edge technology. How could I? – I owe my life to it, literally.

But I feel technology should be our friend and ally, making us all more comfortable – not a jagged-edged, juggernaut jailor keeping us enslaved in its unrelenting power.

November 1 – Yesterday was my friend Jane Marshall's birthday. In truth, she's more of an acquaintance as I don't know her all that well, but she's always seemed to be a really sweet and lovely person – popular and difficult not to like. She certainly deserves a mention here.

It was also, of course, Halloween and Sam and Carl threw a fancy dress party to mark the occasion. Very good it was, too.

Sam loves hosting such events and really goes to town, doing a grand job in buying lots of cheap but effective decorations and spending hours putting them up. Hers was the only house in their street with pumpkins and paraphernalia outside as well as in.

Various mates joined Sam, Carl, Bec, Rudy, Bailey and Albert the dog for the shindig, including Jem Hannen, Tina Mcauley, Sonia Jamieson, Andy Frend, Jimmy and his daughter Molly.

Sam's cousin Jac brought her terrier pup over from New Milton to join us and Kelly Adams popped in briefly with her daughter Storm and niece Jade. They then went off to the Bell, where Storm apparently won first prize in the pub's fancy dress contest.

November 5 – Gunpowder, treason and plot are looking like increasingly attractive propositions right now with this cold-hearted shower in charge. I'm joking of course!

Terrorism will never ever be the right way to bring about the radical change we so desperately need. All that does is replace one oppressive regime with another. Transforming the current system into a proper democracy is the best option I see.

But we do need to get rid of these coalition cut-throats and their brutal and biased cash-crazy policies as soon as possible. Roll on next May's general election.

Turning to more personal matters, I had my annual heart check-up at the Royal Bournemouth Hospital today. So far, so good – phew!

Dr Rozkovec, my consultant, re-iterated the fact that my replacement tissue valve is leaking but said the leak hadn't worsened. If it does, or the valve deteriorates too much, I might need surgery again. But for now it's see you again next November.

AFC Bournemouth – the Cherries – sit proudly atop the Championship football league after a 2-0 away win over Sheffield Wednesday last night.

My adopted home town team are on fire at the moment. They recently won 8-0 away at Birmingham in a league match and beat Premier League team West Brom in the League Cup knockout competition to line up a mouth-watering quarter-final tie at home to Liverpool. Fantastic!

Another fast subject change brings me on to that book *SOS – Alternatives to Capitalism*, which I've now finished.

I've found it an excellent read. I've always known in my heart of hearts that the harsh, cash and competition obsessed form of capitalism I've grown up and grown old with is wrong. Seriously, morally and spiritually.

But I've been equally put off by the hard line form of socialism widely and traditionally regarded as the only alternative. It's constantly been just as pre-occupied with capital, material things and a payment-for work way of operating.

And it's been just as cavalier in its treatment of our environment and its resources as commodities to be exploited by humans.

But the urgent need to reverse this trend or see our planet die – and us with it – has led to a priority review that started in the 1960s and continues to become increasingly relevant and vital.

Swift begins by returning to the days before cash-worship capitalism took hold – when there was far more of a communal vibe going on with commons land and common wealth for use by all.

Both were then ruthlessly fenced off as the concepts of private property and private resources took over from the practices of public ownership and access and the gap between the haves and have-nots became steadily wider.

Cash was crowned king, bankers got rich and financial institutions emerged as global power blocks as hard line capitalism and then hard-edged communism vied for supremacy in an increasingly materialistic and spiritually bankrupt world.

Growth became the buzzword of all political parties as Mother Earth's resources were brutally and recklessly exploited in a mad consumerist drive.

Then, in the middle of the last century, people started realizing the high costs of all this, both in terms of our precious environment and the poor quality of life of humans.

The truth dawned that we couldn't infinitely plunder a finite world without destroying our own support network, threatening our own survival.

Swift explores a range of radical concepts with refreshing humour and compassion – including eco-socialism, democratic socialism, anarchism and the radical new idea of adopting a degrowth plan.

This doesn't mean going back to primitive living – it's a lot more about slowing materialistic development to re-focus and reprioritize using a more environment-friendly, community-based, truly democratic and caring approach.

All this dovetails nicely with my own vision of a future governed by green principles and grass-roots decision making where wealth is distributed a lot more fairly, everyone gets a basic income to feed, clothe and house themselves and hard line cash-crazy self-centred policies give way to a more caring and spiritual approach.

This seems to be the practical crystallization of the vague hippy dream from the late 1960s. That's why I passionately advocate it.

I've been a firm believer in all these principles for a while now, but I've not known how they could be achieved. Swift's book shows ways in which these ideals could be realized – or at least aspired to. I'd thoroughly recommend it.

He borrows several quotations including a Japanese proverb – vision without action is a daydream, action without vision is a nightmare. I like that.

November 6 – Thoroughly enjoyed a lovely bonfire and fireworks party last night with Sam, Carl, Rudy, Bailey, Bec, Russell, Tina, Jem, Andy and Jimmy. Sweet!

November 7 – Stroppy David Cameron's at it again – picking fights with people that is. Apparently bored with slagging off immigrants and Islamists, he's now turned his vitriolic attention to our European allies.

He's bluntly refusing to cough up a £2 billion bill suddenly slapped on Britain by the EU executive with a December 1 deadline.

It's apparently the price we're paying for our success.

The budget contribution demand has seemingly derived from an alleged better than expected performance by the British economy over the past four years. Some countries are getting similar bills while others, including France, receive rebates.

Well, several thoughts immediately occur to me. Firstly, on the surface, it appears grossly unfair to be penalized for apparent success in managing our economy better than others.

Secondly, it's a bit bloody rich for Cameron to bleat on now when Conservative, Labour and now coalition governments have all been so eager for over 40 years to tie us more and more closely to Europe and its oppressive edicts over-riding domestic policies and legislation.

He resembles a belligerent schoolboy taking back his ball and storming off in a huff because he doesn't like the rules of a game he's been quite happy and willing to play until he started losing.

The same applies to the immigration policies and human rights laws he's also recently challenged.

Cameron says he's making a stand for his country. I'd say it's a bit late to try and paint himself as a champion of the electorate he's viciously screwed and arrogantly disregarded up to now. Anyone would think there's an election next spring!

It's also far too late for politicians to start moaning about European rules and talking about referendums about pulling out of the Union. Why weren't they saying all this years ago, before signing treaty after treaty getting us more and more involved?

To try and extricate ourselves now would have massive implications for our economy, possibly sending it into a painfully genuine and disastrous tailspin.

There's no doubt that we've benefited in many ways from membership. But there's also been the downside – progressively more interference in our country's running.

My own view is that we're now footing the bill for our political leaders' eagerness to sign away our rights and liberties to the European super-state.

But my over-riding thought is its all bull anyway – rich men in suits waffling about deficits, demands and austerity in a bogus cash-crazed reality where care, common sense, community and spirituality don't feature and you and I matter less and less.

It's a reality I abhor and reject – yet begrudgingly acknowledge that I've little choice but deal with it as I wander through life. Most of the time it's the only consensus paradigm we have, twisted by our leaders with very real, highly damaging results.

I also despise and rail against the razor-edged steel capitalist system woven deeply into that cold sharp reality, and the materialistically-minded politicians using its cruel and heartless principles to win and keep power by pitting us against each other.

Which is why, for now at least, I'm sticking with the Green Party and its spiritually sound manifesto and quest to work within the current uncaring and deeply flawed set-up to transform it from inside into one more eco-friendly and grass-roots democratic.

November 9 (3.30pm) – I was watching the Cenotaph Remembrance Sunday poppy-laying ceremony on telly this morning when I got a text from my son Phil. As a result, I've just spent a lovely few hours with him, Emily and Harvey.

We had coffee at mine then strolled down through Fisherman's Walk to the Café Riva on the cliff top overlooking the sea for a bite to eat before Harvey had a little session in the children's play park nearby – sadly cut short as it started to rain.

It was great seeing the three of them again (Chloe was with Em's parents and Lucas with his mum).

November 11 – I've seen quite a few rock gigs in my time but not that many true icons. Chuck Berry, Bob Dylan, Roy Orbison, Eric Clapton, Frankie Valli, Smokey Robinson and the Who (sadly after Keith Moon's demise) – that's about it.

Or at least it was until last night, when I had the great pleasure and privilege of catching Robert Plant, who in my eyes is right up there with such luminaries.

The former Led Zeppelin front man brought his excellent Sensational Space Shifters band to the O2 Academy in Boscombe. He was in fine form and it was a brilliant show – one of the best I've seen.

He thrilled us with a varied set of new songs, some of his solo material and Zeppelin classics, including What Is and What Should Never Be, Going to California and searing versions of Rock and Roll and Whole Lotta Love.

Being thoroughly entertained by a total legend on your own doorstep – as gigs go, it doesn't really get much better than that!

I went along with Carl Young, Russell Hall, Jem Hannen, Sharon Pendleton, Andy Frend, Debs, Dave and others. What a cracking event!

But it's edging ever closer to 11 am so I'm going to sign off for now, shut down my computer, light a candle and observe a two-minute's silence in remembrance of our war dead. It is, after all, the 100th anniversary year of World War One's outbreak.

November 14 – People often accuse me of being a lightweight. It's a description I wholeheartedly accept and totally embrace.

Even when I was drinking booze seven nights a week, there's no way I could keep up with my mates who were sinking two or three pints to my one. I didn't even attempt it – unlike the silly fools who thought they could and paid the price.

When I hit bad times on benefits, it curtailed my bar attendance and beer consumption big time. In more recent years it's been a matter of preserving my health.

Now I couldn't much give a monkey's what people think. I know my limits and those who can't accept that can pretty much bugger off.

But that doesn't stop me having a bloody good time. Everything in moderation works for me!

November 18 – Last month I said in this journal that it's largely the luck of the draw how and when we leave our current plane of existence. I stick by that – but at the same time I'm not too keen on recklessly hastening my own demise.

Before my heart scare, I didn't much care what junk I threw down my throat, but these days I'm a lot more vigilant over what I put in my body – fatty foods, salt, sugar, alcohol and other potentially harmful substances.

Okay, the faulty valve has been fixed – at least temporarily – but I still have the underlying heart condition, so I'm under doctor's orders to take care of myself, avoid stress and not over-indulge.

I'm constantly at risk of a heart attack or stroke – that's why I'm on daily medication for life and strongly advised to do regular light exercise, eat right, not smoke and not exceed 21 alcohol units a week.

In truth, I don't often manage to have the recommended five a day of fruit and vegetables. I'm fussy and there's a lot I don't like – especially on the fruit front. But most days I have a glass of apple juice and two or three portions of veg.

I steer clear of high-fat products, eat less red meat and have taken up using low-fat meat substitutes, which can be delicious.

I have more turkey, chicken and fish and occasionally have half-fat bacon. I love bacon and don't want to give it up. And I do light exercise three times a week.

Weekends I let this regime slip a fair bit and also drink booze – but being a good boy during the week means I can do so without causing too much harm.

It also means that when it comes to special occasions like Christmas, birthdays and so on I can push my luck and over-indulge slightly without unduly endangering myself.

If I seriously overdid it – like I used to when I smoked, drank seven days a week and scoffed pies and pasties at every opportunity – I'd be asking for trouble.

The funny thing is that when I say such things to some friends, they say I worry too much and point out quite rightly that I could die at the wheels of a bus any day so they recommend I live life to the full.

I see their point – but, like I said, I'm under doctor's orders and don't want to carelessly speed my own departure.

It's also true that some folk die young after heeding all the experts' advice while others play fast and loose yet hang on to a ripe old age – the luck of the draw.

But my heart crisis scared the crap out of me and brutally forced me to confront my own mortality and urgently review my priorities and general take on life.

Now, every extra day I spend here is a bonus, a gift and a blessing. I need to acknowledge that fact and exercise care and caution. But I can still have fun – in a quieter, more relaxed sort of way.

This is what some people just don't get. Why should they? Unless you've faced any kind of dire situation you can't possibly envisage what it's like.

Besides, as I've said before, I haven't so much been given a second chance as a third. To blatantly disrespect that would be both foolish and criminal.

At this juncture I think of a personal anecdote and an old joke.

The anecdote is another true story from my days as a local newspaper journalist.

Whenever anyone in a paper's circulation area reached 100 years old, a reporter and photographer were sent out to interview and take a picture of them.

On one occasion, I was chosen to talk to a centenarian lady at Lymington, Hampshire and get her life story for printing in the *Southern Evening Echo*.

A standard question is how the person concerned has managed to reach their landmark birthday. Usually the reply is along the lines of clean living, no wild parties, eating the right foods, exercising, avoiding excessive alcohol, not smoking and so on.

Such interviews can be tough going because the subject is often frail, hard of hearing and not all that compos mentis.

But this surprisingly alert and sprightly old bird took me aback with her refreshingly different response. "No luv, I used to drink like a fish, smoke like a trooper and have a lot of fun, if you know what I mean. I've had to give it all up now though – pity."

Just goes to show, don't it?

The old joke is the complete reversal of this situation – the same question, but the opposite answer. It's the one about the guy who asks his maiden aunt how she's managed to reach 90.

"Clean living, fresh air and exercise, working hard, being pious and studious, eschewing alcohol, drugs and bad food – generally taking care of myself," she replies.

"So you'd recommend that others do the same then?" muses the nephew.

"God no – I've been bored witless!" she responds.

The anecdote and joke both make salient points. But I'm still intent on looking after myself from now on and avoiding undue risks. The rest I must leave to fickle fortune.

November 19 – When I've fancied playing a bit of music, I've been revisiting my Robert Plant and Led Zeppelin CDs since just prior to his superb Boscombe gig. But I'm now immersing myself in Pink Floyd's excellent new album The Endless River.

I bought it two days ago and have fallen in love with it. Not as commercial sounding as Dark Side of the Moon or as heavy as The Wall, it's a largely instrumental affair reminiscent of the more melodic stuff on Division Bell and Wish You Were Here.

Roger Waters doesn't feature, having left the group in 1985, but it's still unmistakably Floyd. Dave Gilmour and Nick Mason both appear and so does Richard Wright – prominently but sadly posthumously.

The keyboardist and founder member died in 2008 and this is seen as a fitting tribute to him as well as the band's "swan song" album.

Floyd's 15th studio set and first offering of new material since The Division Bell 20 years ago, it's sat proudly atop the UK album charts since the day of its release last week and is also number one in several other countries.

Yes, there are still millions of Pink Floyd fans about, including me. They're my third favourite group of all time behind the Beatles and Led Zeppelin. I love them so much I actually place them above the Who and the Rolling Stones.

November 20 – I said yesterday that each day is a blessing. This is how I feel in my current circumstances. No doubt I'd see things differently if I were in severe pain, starving to death or being viciously persecuted or tortured. I feel for those who are.

Now, to finish this bit, I'll leave you with the following thought. Wealth and resources are available – its how they're controlled and distributed that governs who's well off and who's struggling, who lives and who dies.

****

CHAPTER EIGHT – TRUTH SEEKER

November 20, four hours later – I consider myself a truth seeker in a world of lies and twisted realities, burning questions and puzzling inconsistencies.

So I'm intrigued when I watch telly programmes like the two I found on catch-up TV in the gap between my journal entry of earlier today and this one.

They were from a Yesterday channel series called Forbidden History, hosted by Jamie Theakston. The first was about the Illuminati and the second about the alleged descendants of Jesus.

Are the Illuminati the good guys or the bad guys? Was Jack the Ripper a member and is American rapper Jay-Z among the organisation's willing modern-day servants?

And did Jesus – or more correctly, Y'shua bar Yosef – survive crucifixion to marry Mary Magdalene and establish a royal bloodline that survives to this day?

I don't know and very few can say one way or the other with any degree of certainty. But of one thing I am convinced – throughout the ages there have been ruthless and unscrupulous individuals deliberately muddying the waters, using situations to further their own agendas and ambitions.

So it both amuses and annoys me when people declare things boldly and arrogantly as absolute truth when they have no way of proving it.

Yes, we can believe what we like, have unshakable faith even. And when it comes to spiritual validation we have to trust that our inner hearts know what's right and wrong, true and false – provided we're properly tuned in to our higher selves, that is.

But in our fractured and flawed so-called reality it's nigh on impossible to decide with any confidence who's giving it to us straight and who's fibbing or elaborating. It's been that way for millennia as masters of manipulation have constantly played us all.

Pop stars, political leaders and even popes have been caught on camera apparently using Illuminati hand signs. Critics say these are by implication satanic gestures.

Well, I 'm not sure about the pontiffs and politicians, but I suspect pop people who use these signs and put Illuminati symbolism in their stage, shows, videos and photos are just teasing us and having a bit of fun after learning of the whole Illuminati/New World Order debate.

I could be wrong. I might be right. I dunno – do you?

November 21 – The United Kingdom Independence Party has its second MP at Westminster after Mark Reckless won yesterday's Rochester and Strood by-election.

He took 16,867 votes, 2,920 more than Conservative Kelly Tolhurst's 13,947, with Labour's Naushabah Khan coming third on 6,713. Green Party candidate Clive Gregory was fourth with 1,692 votes.

Once again the real losers getting a right pasting were the Lib Dems – fifth with only 349, their lowest vote total in a by-election.

Mr Reckless, whose defection from the Tories to UKIP triggered the contest in Kent, later travelled to London to take his seat in Parliament.

Oh dear! I sincerely hope this is just a protest vote against the coalition government and not an indication that UKIP are becoming a real force to be reckoned with.

It seems many people are attracted to UKIP because they're fed up with far too many Eastern Europeans flocking to our shores and the EU's overbearing control over immigration policies, our domestic issues and our legal system.

I have a degree of sympathy with both points. And I actually support one or two of their policies – notably the proposed scrapping of the costly HS2 rail link plan.

But they also want to leave the EU completely, legalise handguns, repatriate migrants, blow up wind farms and ban HIV positive people from entering the country.

I'm deeply worried that behind the smooth and appealing rhetoric lies a hard line right-wing agenda intent on dismantling the welfare system, privatising the NHS, ignoring green concerns and victimising gay people and ethnic minorities.

I'm also fearful that the party will become a haven for bigoted, nasty, intolerant and even mentally unhinged individuals with seriously suspect, very dark motives.

I'm pleased with the Greens' continued rise and feel the total collapse in support for the Lib-Dems is exactly what they deserve after their leaders blew a rare chance to exercise real power by instead caving in disgracefully to cruel, unfair Tory policies.

November 22 – Happy birthday to my son Phil, 25 today. Hoping he has a great time.

November 23 – Some people have really sick minds.

I find it both disturbing and very sad that whenever anyone establishes a reputation for being a kind, decent person bringing joy to the world, there's always someone else lurking in the shadows determined to destroy it.

These bitter, twisted liabilities are never happier than when they're having a pop at those far more deserving of praise and admiration than they are.

Politicians, bullies and others who make careers out of inflicting pain and division have arguably asked for such treatment. But some of those targeted haven't.

Granted, none of us is whiter than white and we've all strayed from the path on occasions. But whether you believe in karma or you see Saint Peter weighing up your good acts against your bad at the Pearly Gates, it's all a question of balance.

Those who have led lives packed with good, altruistic words and deeds can later be exposed as having also committed unspeakable acts along the way.

Conversely, some who have done really terrible things in the past, maybe even served time in jail for them, can turn it around quite spectacularly and end up being a generally positive force benefiting others.

I firmly hold that the Universe has its own natural scales of justice, balancing out individuals' virtues and defects in determining their fates in this life and beyond, no matter what their beliefs – reincarnation, Heaven and Hell, Elysian Fields or Nirvana.

I also feel strongly that there's far too much dark negativity and blatant hypocrisy infecting many people's attitudes and rash declarations about others' behaviour.

November 24 – Another family birthday, this time concerning my sister Carol. Happy 68th sis, hope you have a super one!

November 27 – I've been reading some more on that Illuminati website. As I've already stated, I initially thought it spoke a lot of sense and I agreed with much of what was being said. I still do, but I'm becoming increasingly anxious about the kind of society it ultimately envisages.

I concur with the view expressed that the world's great religions are seriously flawed and cause division and bitter clashes that can escalate into bloody violence.

I agree that these belief systems rely far too much on blind faith in preference to spiritual knowledge – gnosis – and true enlightenment.

I hold that positive and negative impulses reside within us all, entangled in a constant tussle for supremacy, and some can become driven by the dark energy flow, making them appear evil, while others are guided by the light, ending up virtuous and deeply spiritual individuals apparently imbued with divinity.

But I stop short of the Illuminati's contentions that they themselves are the only enlightened ones and humans can become godlike if they follow suit.

I fully support their apparent hatred of harsh cash-driven capitalism and our current system where some enjoy great wealth and privilege while others live rough, starve and die. I agree that's immoral.

And I like what they say about replacing an economic regime where people do jobs they probably hate just to pay the bills with a new one based on work that actually fulfils individuals' potential, giving them real satisfaction.

But I've already said I'd oppose the ousting of democracy in favour of a meritocracy and I've questioned where the mentally-challenged would fit into such a set-up.

And I'm deeply concerned by the whole cold, clinical, harsh and soulless tone of the Illuminati vision, where mathematics, logic, reason, intellect and science dominate and all religions and even the concept of love itself are jettisoned as inherently evil.

No, I think I'll stick with love, peace and harmony thank you – and my opinion that, while deeply flawed and warped by human ambition and prejudice, rigid dogma and blatant propaganda, the world's biggest religions all contain bright flashes of insight and great jewels of wisdom.

So do paganism, Egyptian, Greek, Persian, Chinese and other millennia-old systems and the ancient nature-based faiths that often show a more profound grasp of eternal truths than any of them.

It's our task to extract the facts from the lies and spin using our inbuilt instincts to decide for ourselves what feels right or wrong – and not rely too heavily on others to provide the answers.

Yes, I still want the corrupt and hostile old world order overturned, or at least transformed into something more caring and mutually supportive. But I've come to the conclusion that the system proposed on that Illuminati website isn't the answer.

November 29 – I've had a grand couple of days. Yesterday, Carol and David came over from Selsey for our traditional pre-Christmas meal and present exchange with Suzette. As usual, we had a Toby Carvery lunch at Fleetsbridge near Poole.

Then, at tea-time, I strolled up to Sam and Carl's for another booze and chat session with them, Becca, Diane, Tina Mcauley and Jimmy. Bec's adorable terrier dog Albert was there and we saw Rudy and Bailey briefly before they went to bed.

Today I had another meal out, this time with Phil, Emily and Chloe. They came over from Ferndown for coffee and a catch-up before we went for lunch at a Harvester restaurant near Cooper Dean roundabout.

It was lovely bright weather so we then went for a stroll through Fisherman's Walk where Chloe loved seeing the squirrels as proud dad Phil snapped away with his camera. He's really got into photography of late and has taken some super shots showing he has a talent for it.

But while I've been having a super time, things in the outside world are as serious and tragic as ever.

Today is the 13th anniversary of George Harrison's passing. I lit a candle for him earlier and put a little tribute on Facebook.

Cricket fans are in mourning following the shock death of 25-year-old Australian batsman Phillip Hughes in a freak accident.

He died in hospital on Thursday, two days after being struck on the top of the neck by a ball during a domestic match in Sydney. He never regained consciousness.

Hughes, who also played for Hampshire, Middlesex and Worcestershire, was hit by a delivery from bowler Sean Abbott, who is understandably devastated.

Dozens of people have died in a gun and bomb attack during prayers at one of the biggest mosques in the northern Nigerian city of Kano.

Many more people have been hurt, with one rescue official putting casualty figures at almost 400.

The Central Mosque is where influential Muslim leader the Emir of Kano, usually leads the prayers. He recently urged people to arm themselves against Islamist militant group Boko Haram.

No organisation has yet admitted responsibility, but it's widely assumed that Boko Haram was behind the atrocity.

At home, PM David Cameron has announced that people coming to the UK from other EU countries will have to wait four years before receiving certain welfare payments.

He apparently sees this as a way of deterring jobless foreigners from flocking to our shores, putting a strain on our benefits system.

It will also, of course, help win back wavering Tory voters attracted by Nigel Farage and his UKIP chums' bold claims that theirs is the only party serious about challenging the EU and wresting back control over runaway immigration.

I've already placed on record my concern at the huge numbers of folk coming over from Eastern Europe by order of the EU. This isn't racist, it's common sense.

There's no doubt that Cameron's latest pronouncement will be very popular and I do think it's wrong that immigrants can claim benefits immediately they arrive here, before they've even paid any money into our system.

But four years? – That seems excessively harsh to me.

And, as always, I suspect the PM's motives – in this case, I see a cynical bid to save cash while appeasing jittery right-wing Tories who would otherwise defect to UKIP.

December 1 – Earlier today I played an Elvis Costello CD. I'd forgotten what a brilliant lyric writer he is. He has a wonderful way with the English language and his imaginative, intelligent and evocative wordplay is a joy to behold.

Another great song wordsmith is Black Sabbath's bass player Geezer Butler. I was similarly reminded of this when I listened to a CD by the heavy rockers the other day. Totally different in style to Costello, he is similarly skilled in the art of lyric writing. Ozzy Osbourne's not bad either.

In fact, the pop and rock world is full of good lyricists, from oldies like Chuck Berry, Bob Dylan, Bernie Taupin, Joni Mitchell, Peter Sinfield, Cat Stevens, Kate Bush, Roger Waters, Dolly Parton, David Bowie, Pete Townsend, David Gates, Ray Davies, Bruce Springsteen, Lemmy, Stevie Wonder and Paul Simon to bright newer stars such as Noel Gallagher, Eminem, Alex Turner, Ed Sheeran, Rita Ora, Ellie Goulding, Kate Nash and Mike Rosenberg (Passenger).

Plus of course, John Lennon, George Harrison and Paul McCartney. Yeah, them again!

As a lyric writer myself, I dream of reaching such heights of excellence as those displayed by the Beatle boys, Costello, Butler or any of the aforementioned.

I love good music with good words. You may have also gathered that I love watching telly too. And my fave programme at the moment is I'm a Celebrity Get Me Out of Here.

This year's crop of hopeful kings and queens of the jungle includes actress Vicky Michelle, ex-footballer Jimmy Bullard, former politician Edwina Currie, TV presenter Mel Sykes and Carl Fogarty, the most successful World Superbike racer of all time.

Ant and Dec's ITV One show is highly watchable, but I actually prefer the ITV Two programme with Laura Whitmore and former jungle king Joe Swash. It's more relaxed, funnier and has revealing film footage of the campmates not shown on One.

December 2 – Last night I went with my mate Carl to see Saxon at Boscombe's O2 Academy. And Biff and the boys were great – just as good as when I caught them over three decades ago at Poole.

Wheels of Steel indeed! Hard and heavy, loud and fast rock and roll does it for me every time. Fabulous!

December 4 – Yesterday would have been Jim Excell's birthday had he still been alive. So his daughter, my good friend Sam, invited me to hers to mark the occasion with a drink or three.

Carl, Becca and Tina Mcauley were there and the boys Rudy and Bailey too for a short while before going to bed. Rich Jeffery popped in briefly.

December 7 – I went to the Bell last night to celebrate guv'nor Mark Evans' birthday, but left when it got a bit too busy for my liking.

Apart from Mark and his lady Laura Williams, I also saw John Gaynor, Billy Clarkson, Kelly Adams, Matt Brandt, Dani Knight, Rebecca Browning, Chris Davis, Dawn Lewis with her mate Penny, and Sam and Dave Lowney. Cool!

Today is a very sad anniversary that should have been a very happy one. Its 26 years since my first son John was stillborn. I've lit a candle for him while wondering what might have been.

Twenty-six years – it doesn't seem that long, and the pain still burns. But the bitter heartbreak turned to tears of joy 11 and a half months later when Joe gave birth to our second son Philip.

Phil, just 25, has been the one constant source of joy in my life ever since and of course I now have my grandchildren Chloe, Lucas and Harvey plus Emily and my newly-extended family to continue putting icing on the cake.

Changing the subject, I feel it's time for a bit of philosophy. Some say money's the root of all evil. No I'm not! – And besides, they're wrong, seriously misquoting a Biblical reference that actually says the love of money is the root of all kinds of evil.

Now that, my friends, is much closer to the truth. Money can be used for good or bad purposes. It can save lives as well as destroy them.

December 8 – RIP John Lennon, shot dead by a deranged former fan outside his New York apartment on December 8, 1980. There's some right sickos in this world, aren't there? I'm off shopping soon so I'll light a candle for John when I get back.

So former World Superbike champion Carl Fogarty is the new "king of the jungle." He emerged victorious as the annual I'm a Celebrity Get Me out of Here reality TV show reached its climax yesterday.

Singer Jake Quickenden, who recently made a name for himself by appearing on the X-Factor, was runner-up and TV presenter Melanie Sykes, of Des and Mel fame, came third as viewers voted for their 2014 jungle monarch.

I was chuffed that Mel got into the final but disappointed that she didn't take the crown as she was my first choice from the start of the three-week competition.

I picked ex-footballer Jimmy Bullard as my runner-up and was shocked and amazed when the larger-than-life amiable joker was the first person voted out. Cool nice guy rapper Tinchy Stryder was my third choice. He came fifth.

Jimmy and Carl quickly formed a really strong bond and became a hilarious double act. "Foggy" was clearly devastated when Jim left but it gave him a chance to shine in his own right and he grew on me as the series progressed.

He came over as a sound as a pound bloke – determined and fearless when doing the nasty trials and a strong, sturdy, reliable campmate. He was also funny and at times endearingly modest and emotional.

In the end, he proved to be a very worthy winner – hugely liked by both his jungle buddies and the public.

December 10 – Yippee! *Sunshine and Ice, Volume Seven, Persistent Illusions*, is out on Kindle and in paperback form. I received my copies through the post yesterday afternoon.

Now I await the final proofs of *Volume Eight, Patience and Wisdom* so I can amend and approve them pending publication of that, too.

And volumes one to six are once again available in both formats thanks to my new publishers, Author Essentials of Falmer, East Sussex. Sweet!

I noticed something yesterday evening while flicking through a paperback version of *Persistent Illusions*.

In a journal entry written last Christmas Eve, I referred to my little flat here as "my home of 30 years." Oops! – I should have said 20 of course, now 21.

I never have been very good at maths!

December 14 – Congratulations to Samantha Jones, my mate Tom's daughter, on the birth of her baby boy.

Yesterday I had my annual festive drinks and catch-up session with Lea, the lady I used to work with at Southbourne's Red Cross charity shop. Very nice it was too.

As usual, we met up at Boscombe Conservative Club, where she's a member, and spent a few hours sharing news, having a laugh and putting the world to rights.

With the festive season well and truly upon us and various special events marking the centenary of World War One's outbreak, our thoughts turn to the famous Christmas truce, now being topically highlighted again.

Sainsbury's have even got in on the act with a poignant and moving advert about the true story of British and German troops defying their overlords and leaving the trenches in 1914 to meet in no-man's land for carol singing, present exchanging and at least one game of football.

It just goes to show the total madness and absurdity of warfare and the burning desire of the human spirit to seek unity and peace rather than division and bloodshed.

The temporary ceasefire, or series of ceasefires according to some accounts, was all too brief and hostilities were soon resumed, to drag on for another four years.

We've also just marked the 34th anniversary of John Lennon's assassination in New York on December 8, 1980.

Radios are again playing his seasonal classic song Happy Xmas (War is Over), which features a choir of children singing his lyric "war is over if you want it."

How topical and appropriate this is in light of both the WW1 centenary and publicity over that legendary truce.

I'm with you John. Peace is within grasp if we all want it enough.

And on that optimistic note I shall begin to bring this volume of my life journal to a close.

****

CHAPTER NINE – SPARKLY MOMENTS

December 14, continued – I've had many reasons to smile this year.

Being reunited with Tom and Chris Jones was brilliant and hooking up with our old mate Steve Gray was an added bonus.

There was also the Bell re-launch, the Gary Numan, Saxon and Robert Plant gigs, those few days in Weymouth and several super barbeques, special event parties and booze and silliness sessions at Sam and Carl's with them, their family, pets and pals.

I've had a number of brandy coffees and good laughs with my great buddy Jem and some fine times at the pub with a variety of chums. I've also spent wonderful hours with Phil, Emily and my grandchildren.

Then there was that lovely pre-Christmas meal and catch-up with Carol, David and Suzette.

Furthermore, I've savoured sweet walks to the cliff top to sit overlooking the sea, bought and played some terrific music on CDs, watched a lot of top notch TV, had my fair share of Facebook fun with family and friends and played my guitar a bit – badly.

Volume Seven of *Sunshine and Ice*, called *Persistent Illusions*, is now out and volumes one to six are once again available after that frustrating publishing hiccup. *Volume Eight – Patience and Wisdom* – will hopefully be out early next year.

And this book, *Volume Nine*, is pretty much finished and ready for submission to my new publishers.

All in all, I've had some right good sparkly moments.

And speaking of sparkling things, the festive season is in full swing now and life's looking pretty good for me, thank goodness.

I don't do New Year resolutions, but I will have to put the brakes on my spending as a matter of urgency once Christmas is out of the way to avoid draining my money resources too much and too soon.

This will probably mean no more holiday breaks and cutting back quite drastically on gig attendances, CD purchases, clothes buying and other little treats. Otherwise I'll be skint again before I know it.

So there you have it – the latest instalment of my life story peppered with lyrics, news, opinions and oddball ramblings.

You may agree with my views, you might not. Either way, that's okay. We're not going to fall out over it, are we?

I tell it as I see it, that's all. Just like anyone else. The only difference is I'm putting it into print and putting it out there.

I guess that just about wraps it up. All that's left is for me to sign off by wishing one and all a very Merry Christmas and a Happy New Year.

Farewell friends – for now at least. Peace and love,

Martin Money
December 14, 2014

****

Each day is a bonus, a gift and a blessing.

Wealth and resources are available – its how they're controlled and distributed that governs who's well off and who's struggling, who lives and who dies.

"Vision without action is a daydream. Action without vision is a nightmare" – Japanese proverb.

This book is dedicated to Phil, Emily, Chloe, Lucas and Harvey;

To Carol, David, their children and grandchildren, Joyce, Suzette, Sandra, Alan and surviving members of the Money clan;

To everyone I've shared love and friendship with, whether still with us or passed on;

And to all seekers of the truth who refuse to accept the status quo as a viable and sustainable option for the future of mankind.

Love and peace people. We're all part of divine Oneness and the time's well ripe for us to accept this and live in harmony with each other, the various species we co-exist with and our precious Mother Earth.

Otherwise, we're doomed. It's a no-brainer, really!

The spark of consciousness called Martin Money.

ABOUT THE AUTHOR

Born in Slough on February 25, 1954, Martin Money lived there until early adulthood, moving to Dorset in 1978.

Leaving school with three A Levels and seven O Levels, he worked in a bank for a few months before starting a 24-year career in regional journalism that ended in redundancy in 1997.

Since then he's had a variety of part-time jobs and also worked as a volunteer for charities.

A proud father and grandfather, he lives in Bournemouth where he enjoys short cliff-top walks, writing, reading, watching TV, listening to music and socialising.

Author's photo by Sam Excell

www.ingramcontent.com/pod-product-compliance
Lightning Source LLC
Chambersburg PA
CBHW062058270326
41931CB00013B/3135